Teacher's Pack

CONTEMPORARY TOPICS

Academic Listening and Note-Taking Skills

THIRD EDITION

David Beglar
Neil Murray

Michael Rost
SERIES EDITOR

PEARSON
Longman

Contemporary Topics 3: Advanced
Academic Listening and Note-Taking Skills
Third Edition

Pearson Education, 10 Bank Street, White Plains, NY 10606

Staff credits: The people who made up the *Contemporary Topics 3* team, representing editorial, production, design, and manufacturing, are Rhea Banker, Danielle Belfiore, Dave Dickey, Christine Edmonds, Nancy Flaggman, Dana Klinek, Amy McCormick, Linda Moser, Carlos Rountree, Jennifer Stem, Leigh Stolle, Paula Van Ells, Kenneth Volcjak, and Pat Wosczyk.
Cover design: Ann France
Text composition: ElectraGraphics, Inc.
Text font: 11/13 Times

ISBN-10: 0-13-600513-6
ISBN-13: 978-0-13-600513-1

PEARSON LONGMAN ON THE WEB

Pearsonlongman.com offers online resources for teachers and students. Access our Companion Websites, our online catalog, and our local offices around the world.

Visit us at **www.pearsonlongman.com**.

Printed in the United States of America
6 7 8 9 10—V036—14 13 12 11 10

CONTENTS

INTRODUCTION

The *Contemporary Topics* series provides a stimulating, content-based approach that helps students develop their listening, note-taking, and discussion skills while studying relevant topics. Each unit centers around a short academic lecture, with topics drawn from a range of disciplines.

The lectures feature engaging instructors with live student audiences, and take place in authentic lecture hall settings. The multimodal design of each lecture allows for various learning formats for DVD users, including audio- or video-only presentations, optional subtitling, Presentation Points slide support, and pop-up Coaching Tips.

In order to maximize the benefits of content-based instruction, the *Contemporary Topics* series has developed a carefully sequenced eight-step learning methodology. This introduction provides an overview of each of these steps.

Step 1: Connect to the Topic   *Estimated Time: 10 minutes*

This opening section invites students to activate what they already know about the unit topic by connecting it to their own experiences and beliefs. Typically, students fill out a short survey and compare answers with a partner. The teacher acts as a facilitator, having students share ideas about the topic before they explore it further.

Basic Procedure:

- Set the tone for the unit by talking about the image(s) on the page or related current news events.

- Read the introductory paragraph aloud, paraphrasing as necessary.

- Have students complete the survey/activity.

- Ask students to compare answers with a partner, or discuss answers casually as a class.

Methodology Focus: The actual content of students' responses in this initial activity is not as important as their attempt to understand and interact. It is important that all students participate in activating their ideas about the theme of the unit. This engagement helps set the tone of "active listening" throughout the unit. Having students compare answers with a partner helps ensure that every student is on task and thinking about the unit topic.

 ## Step 2: Build Your Vocabulary   *Estimated Time: 15 minutes*

This section familiarizes students with the key content words and phrases from the lecture. Each lecture contains 10–15 key words from the Academic Word List to ensure that students learn core vocabulary needed for academic success. Students read and *listen to* target words in context so that they can better prepare for the upcoming lecture. Students then complete exercises to get an initial understanding of the target lexis of the unit. Interact with Vocabulary! is a supplementary activity that focuses on the syntax and collocations of new vocabulary in the unit.

Basic Procedure:

- Have students listen to the sentences or paragraphs.

- Have students guess the meaning of each boldfaced word and choose the best definition.

- If time permits, try the Interact with Vocabulary! activity to enable students to focus on form as they learn new words and collocations.

Methodology Focus: Vocabulary knowledge and the ability to recognize vocabulary as it is spoken are key predictors of listening comprehension. As such, spending some pre-listening time on recognizing key vocabulary from the lecture will usually increase students' comprehension of the ideas in the lecture. It's best to spend 10–15 minutes on vocabulary preparation. More than this may give students the impression that vocabulary learning is overly important. Research shows that multiple exposures to new words in context is necessary for vocabulary acquisition, so it's not essential that students "master" the vocabulary in this section. Frequent reviews of the vocabulary sections will aid in acquisition.

Step 3: Focus Your Attention   *Estimated Time: 10 minutes* In this section,
students learn strategies for listening actively and taking clear notes. Because a major part of "active listening" involves a readiness to deal with comprehension difficulties, this section provides specific tips to help students direct their attention and gain more control of how they listen. The Try It Out! section, based on a short audio extract, allows students to work on listening and note-taking strategies before they get to the main lecture. Typically, examples of actual notes are provided to give students concrete "starter models."

Basic Procedure:

- Go through this section carefully, reading explanations aloud. Draw attention to examples.

- Play the audio for Try It Out! in order to have students experience the given technique.

- After you play the audio extract once or twice, have students compare answers and/or notes with a partner.

Methodology Focus: Active listening involves a number of component strategies for focusing students' attention: predicting, guessing (i.e. using available knowledge to make good guesses), filling in gaps and making connections, monitoring areas where they don't understand, asking questions, and responding personally. Above all, active listening involves curiosity and a desire to understand more deeply. This section provides tips for focusing students' attention that, when learned incrementally, will help them become more active listeners. It is important that students find a specific way to control their attention and concentration as they listen.

Step 4: Listen to the Lecture   *Estimated Time: 20–30 minutes* As the central
section of each unit, Listen to the Lecture allows for two full listening cycles: one to focus on "top-down listening" strategies (Listen for Main Ideas) and one to focus on "bottom-up listening" strategies (Listen for Details). In keeping with the principles of content-based instruction, students are provided with several layers of support. In the Before You Listen section, students are guided to activate concepts and vocabulary they already know or studied earlier in the unit.

The lecture can be viewed in video mode or just listened to in audio mode. In video mode, the lecture can be accompanied by the speaker's Presentation Points or by subtitles for reinforcing comprehension (recommended as a final review). Coaching Tips on strategies for listening, note-taking, and critical thinking can also be turned on.

Basic Procedure:

Before You Listen

- Have students go through this section explicitly—for instance, actually writing down a "prediction" when asked.

Listen for Main Ideas

- Have students *close their books* and take notes as they listen.
- Play the lecture through or pause at times. If pausing, it's best to do so at episode boundaries (see Audioscripts in this Teacher's Pack), as these are natural pausing points.
- Have students complete the exercise, working alone, using their notes.
- Check answers, or play the lecture again so students can confirm their answers. If repeating the lecture, have students confirm and expand their notes with books closed.

Listen for Details

- Play the lecture one more time, again with students confirming and expanding their notes. Then have students complete the Listen for Details exercise.

Methodology Focus: The lecture itself is the focal point of each unit, and therefore the focal point of the content-based approach. In this approach, students of course learn grammar, vocabulary, and pronunciation, but always within the context of relevant content, which may make it more memorable. We recommend that you focus on helping students understand the content of each lecture as deeply as possible, and work on specific language skills during the Talk about the Topic, Review Your Notes, and Extend the Topic sections. To better understand the lecture, students can work on two kinds of exercises: "Top-down listening" generally refers to "getting the gist" of what is said, not focusing on all of the details. "Bottom-up listening" generally refers to hearing "the signal"—that is, the exact words, intonations, and syntax that a speaker uses. Effective listening involves both kinds of processing. As teachers, we may naturally assume that "top-down" processing is more important, but research shows that skills in bottom-up processing is *a key determiner of progress* in L2 listening.

 Step 5: Talk about the Topic *Estimated Time: 15 min* Here students gain valuable discussion skills as they talk about the lecture. Discussion skills are an important part of academic success, and most students benefit from structured practice. In these activities, students listen to a short "model discussion" involving both native and non-native speakers, and identify the speaking strategies and gambits that are used. They then attempt to use some of those strategies in their own discussion groups.

Basic Procedure:

- Have students close their books and listen to the discussion.
- With books open, students may listen again and complete Parts A and B to show a basic understanding of the discussion. Alternatively, you can have students answer general comprehension questions: What was this discussion about? What happened in this discussion? etc.

- Next, have students work in groups of three to five, ideally. They should choose a topic and discuss. They should try to use the discussion strategies they have learned in this or previous units.

Methodology Focus: The first two activities in this section are awareness-raising: We want students to understand the content of the discussion *and* try to identify the types of "discourse strategies" that the study group students are using to make the discussion go well. Discussion ability involves a combination of verbal and nonverbal skills. If showing the video, encourage students to focus on the nonverbal actions of the student speakers: their body language (posture), gaze (direction of eyes on other speakers), and back-channeling (signals to show they are paying attention). Speaking strategies develop incrementally. It's important to have students try out different types of strategies in order to see how they may or may not help students express themselves more fully.

Step 6: Review Your Notes *Estimated Time: 15 minutes* Using notes for review

and discussion is an important study skill that is developed in this section. Students are guided in reviewing the content of the unit, clarifying concepts, and preparing for the Unit Test. Incomplete, abbreviated examples of actual notes are provided to help students not only review for the test but also compare and improve their own note-taking skills.

Basic Procedure:

- Have students take out their notes and, with a partner, *take turns* explaining the ideas from the lecture.

- Then have them complete the partial notes.

- Ask if there are any questions about the lecture or anything in their notes. You may wish to preview the Unit Test to be sure that students have discussed the items that will be on it.

Methodology Focus: This section "completes the loop" on note-taking. Research shows that the value of note-taking for memory building is realized primarily when note-takers review their notes and attempt to reconstruct the content. By making explicit statements about the content of the lecture, students are "pushing" their output. They need to use precise grammar and vocabulary in order to articulate their ideas.

 ## Step 7: Take the Unit Test *Estimated Time: 15 minutes* This activity completes the

study cycle of the unit: preparation, listening to the lecture, review of content, and assessment. The Unit Test, contained only in this Teacher's Pack, is to be photocopied and distributed by the teacher. Students complete it in class as they listen to the test questions on the audio CD. The *Contemporary Topics* tests are challenging—intended to motivate students to learn the material thoroughly. The format features an answer sheet with choices; the question "stem" is provided on audio only. Test-taking skills include verbatim recall, paraphrasing, inferencing, and synthesizing information from parts of the lecture.

Basic Procedure:

- Optional: Play the lecture once again.

- Pass out a copy of the Unit Test to each student and go over the directions.

- Play the audio for the test one time as students complete the test by circling their answers. You may pause the audio between questions.

- Collect the tests to correct yourself, or have students exchange papers and go over the answers in class. Replay the audio as you go over the correct answers.

Methodology Focus: The tests in *Contemporary Topics* have the question "stem" on audio only—the students can't read it. They have to listen carefully and then choose the correct answer. This format is more challenging than most standardized tests, such as the TOEFL. We chose this challenging format to motivate students to work through the unit diligently and know the content well.

 Step 8: Extend the Topic *Estimated time: 20 minutes* This final section creates a natural extension of the unit topic to areas that are relevant to students. Students first listen to a supplementary media clip drawn from a variety of interesting genres. Typically, students then have a discussion or prepare a class presentation.

Basic Procedure:

- Choose one of the activities, or more if time permits. Review the steps of the activity together.

- Allow time, if possible, for student presentations.

Methodology Focus: An important aspect of a content-based approach is the application, or follow-up step. This step helps students personalize the content of the unit, choosing to develop topics of personal interest. Allowing time for student research and presentations not only increases interest and involvement in the course, but also allows the teacher an opportunity to give individualized feedback that will help students' progress.

By completing these eight steps, students can develop stronger listening, speaking, and note-taking skills and strategies—thereby becoming more confident and independent learners.

Michael Rost
Series Editor

Multimedia Guidelines: With the DVD, you can play the lecture in different modes: video, video with subtitles, video with Coaching Tips, video with Presentation Points, video with Coaching Tips and subtitles, and video with Coaching Tips and Presentation Points. We do not recommend playing the video with both the Presentation Points and subtitles on.

Note that while the DVD is compatible with most computer media players, for optimum viewing we suggest playing the DVD on a television screen (ideally a wide-screen), using a DVD player.

You can also play the lecture as audio only, using the CD.

We recommend that you play the lecture once in "plain" video mode, then once as audio only. For review, you can play the video again with the Presentation Points and/or Coaching Tips turned on. As another review option, students can watch the subtitled version on their own.

Viewing preferences can be selected under SET UP. Or, with a remote control, subtitles can be activated at any time using the caption button, and Presentation Points can be activated at any time using the angle button.

UNIT 1 COMMUNICATION STUDIES
Slang and Language Change

UNIT OVERVIEW

In this unit, students will look at the phenomenon of language change, and slang in particular. The lecture will focus on what slang is, its origins, who uses it and why, sources of slang, and attitudes toward it. Toward the end of the unit, students are encouraged to consider the acceptability of slang in certain contexts and to research some slang terms.

Connect to the Topic   *page 2*   *~10 minutes*

As a warm-up activity, consider having students identify the slang term used in the cartoon (*sick*) and its meaning (*really good*). In the survey, students are asked to think of some slang terms they have heard, to guess their meanings, and to use them in a sentence. Students are likely to know the meaning of the slang terms they select, so it's important that they try to guess the meaning of their partner's terms. You may wish to prohibit the use of any potentially offensive terms.

Build Your Vocabulary   *pages 3–4*   *~15 minutes*

Students study the following words and phrases related to communication studies and slang:

adapt to	evolving	inevitable
associated with	exclusive to	integration into
attitudes	expanding	made distinct by
breeds in	experts in	phenomenon
by using	the focus of	reinforces
constantly	identity	widespread
construct	in tune with	

After the Interact with Vocabulary! activity, you may want to have students practice using the boldfaced words with their partners. Knowing collocations can help students expand their vocabularies and increase their fluency.

Focus Your Attention   *page 5*   *~10 minutes*

Students learn about sequence markers in discourse and how these markers can help them to distinguish different ideas and better organize their notes:

To start/begin with, . . .	*Next, . . .*	*Another point/idea . . .*
First, . . . ; Second, . . . ; Third, . . .	*Then . . .*	*Last, . . .*
	Moving on . . .	*Finally, . . .*
	Let's move on to . . .	

Students listen to a short audio clip and practice using sequence markers in their notes.

Listen to the Lecture *pages 6–7* ~*30 minutes*

Students are asked to consider why people use slang (Before You Listen) before listening to the unit lecture on slang. Students then answer true/false items (Listen for Main Ideas) and multiple-choice items (Listen for Details).
Lecture video time: 7 min. 11 sec.   Number of episodes: 10

NOTE

Remember that with the DVD, you can play the lecture in different modes: video, video with subtitles, video with Coaching Tips, video with Presentation Points, video with Coaching Tips and subtitles, and video with Coaching Tips and Presentation Points. (We do not recommend playing the video with both the Presentation Points and subtitles on.) You can also play the lecture as audio only, using the CD. We recommend that you play the lecture once in "plain" video mode, then once as audio only.

Talk about the Topic *page 8* ~*20 minutes*

Four students—Mia, Manny, Hannah, and River—discuss the lecture. Part A focuses on matching these students with questions from the discussion. Note that students are to identify who *answers* the question. In Part B, your students work on these discussion strategies:

- Agreeing: " . . . You're right about that."
- Asking for clarification or confirmation: "Yeah, OK. So what's the confusion?"
- Paraphrasing: "It's a choice, you're saying."

For Part C, students are encouraged to use the discussion strategies they've learned. They may use phrases from the student discussion or come up with their own.
Student discussion video time: 1 min. 56 sec.

Review Your Notes *page 9* ~*15 minutes*

Students focus on reconstructing their notes, paying attention to sequence markers.

BONUS ACTIVITY

As a lead-in to the unit test, you can ask students to deliver an authentic-sounding summary of the complete lecture to their partner using their notes and their own words.

Take the Unit Test *Teacher's Pack page 7* ~*15 minutes*

You may want to play the lecture again just before giving the test. Students answer standard test questions about the content of the lecture. Specifically, the test covers the following: the order in which information is discussed, the definition of slang, the benefits of slang, the lecturer's opinion of slang, and the main idea of the lecture.

Extend the Topic *pages 10–11* ~*30 minutes*

- Listening and Discussion: Students listen to an excerpt about text messaging, then discuss slang in the context of text messaging.
- Reading and Discussion: Students read and discuss three professionals' contrasting attitudes toward slang.
- Research and Presentation: Students conduct additional research on two slang terms, then debate which terms should become "official."

Focus Your Attention:
Try It Out! *page 5*

Speaker: So, we know that people adjust the way they speak for a number of different reasons. First, they simply want to say something about themselves. They want to create a certain impression on whomever it is they're talking to, or perhaps influence them. Then, there's the context. We all change our language according to the situation we're in—where we are and who our audience is. For instance, if we're in an interview, we're going to sound different than if we're chatting with a friend, say. Next, people change their language in order to fit in. When we want to feel accepted by a certain group, we try to speak like the members of that group. And last, there's the entertainment factor: We sometimes adjust the way we speak simply because we can. We are free to play with language and be creative with it—and we enjoy that!

Listen for Main Ideas and Listen
for Details *pages 6–7*

Communication studies lecturer: **E1** The first thing to say about language change is it's inevitable. Language is a living thing, constantly expanding, evolving, and adapting to the humans who use it. We see language change in all areas of language— syntax, phonology, orthography, and semantics. For now, let's just focus on semantics, and on one particular area of semantic change which always grabs people's attention: slang. We all recognize slang, we all use slang. And we use it for a reason. It gives our language a special feel and says something about us. So I'm going to talk a bit about what slang is, who uses it and why, where it comes from, and how it is received. **E2** So what is slang? Here's a definition you might want to jot down: Slang is informal language which tends to be associated with particular groups of people and therefore helps define their identity. Slang often breeds among deprived groups or groups we think of as secretive or underground or nonconforming. Today, though, these associations are becoming much weaker and now everyone uses slang. **E3** So let me home in on this idea of identity as it leads us into the question of why people use slang. A lot of slang comes from people not wanting to be understood by those outside their group. We typically think of using language in order to be understood, but another use of language is to prevent understanding. People use exclusive or private language to give their group a distinct identity. With slang, people can tease one

another, enjoy shared experiences—and keep everyone else at a distance. All cultures have groups or "subcultures" who want to be separate. And yet they want people to know who they are, and what they stand for—and slang helps to construct that identity. **E4** We can say, then, that slang reflects the experiences, beliefs, and values of its speakers. By using the slang associated with a particular social group, you're staking a claim to membership of that group. Being in-group denotes inclusion or acceptance because you play by the group's "rules." Being out-group is the opposite. It's being excluded. Ever notice how non-native speakers are so eager to learn slang even before they have a basic grasp of the language? Well, that's because it's a signal of integration—of membership. "I speak this language, I belong." In a word, slang is cohesive. **E5** Now let's look at the personal benefits of using slang. First, when you use slang well, you show that you're in tune with the times, that you know what is culturally in fashion and you're part of it. Using slang makes you desirable. The second benefit of using slang is that you demonstrate your mastery of the situation— you become an expert. This is because slang is only used in certain settings. And knowing how and when to use it—or when not to use it—gives you a kind of status. **E6** A third benefit of using slang is that it allows you to share social and emotional experiences. So it reinforces your relationships. For example, if you say to your friend, "My new sound system is really safe," you're saying more than just "It's very good." Your use of slang equates sharing an emotional experience. And a fourth benefit of using slang is it's fun. It's often humorous and very creative, like poetry. The semanticist S. I. Hayakawa actually described slang as the "poetry of everyday life." In other words, slang is also a form of play, or entertainment. **E7** So, what are the major inspirations for slang? Well, there are a few that never seem to go out of fashion. I'm talking about love and romance. It's also used for emotional expressions of like and dislike, and you can probably think of dozens of them. These particular slang terms seem to have a pretty short life. They're being replaced by newer words and phrases all the time. And, like I said, if you want to stay cool, you've got to keep up with the changes. **E8** But there's another category of slang term that's really taken off recently, and that's the slang of new technology. Things like personal computers, the Internet, e-mail, and mobile technology. These things have become one of the richest sources of slang, and there are tons of websites designed to celebrate or decode that slang. Here we see certain, often youthful communities, using this to distance themselves from the technologically challenged older generations. **E9** So, we've seen what slang is, who uses it and why, and what inspires it. But what about the present-day attitudes towards it? Well, slang may be widespread and no longer taboo in the way it once was. But that doesn't mean everybody likes it. Some see it as decadent and insist on associating it with groups they see as undesirable or uneducated. They see themselves as guardians of the language and view any kind of change as change for the worse. In my opinion this is absurd. I personally think slang is a sign of life, vibrancy, and beauty in language. As I said at the outset, language is a living thing and will always change. Yet, it seems like people are programmed to view any language change negatively. **E10** OK, so I'd like to summarize now today's main point with a quotation from linguist Tony Thorne, who says, "Slang . . . often performs an important social function, which is to include into or exclude from the intimate circle." So, yes, it may still have negative connotations, but slang is here to stay. It even has taken on an aura of respectability by becoming the subject of serious academic study. And why not? As I've tried to show, it's a fascinating social and linguistic phenomenon.

Coaching Tips

[1] **Listening: Listening for topic signals** The speaker begins the lecture by providing some general information about language change. He then moves from this background information to the specific lecture topic by using several signal phrases. He says: "For now, let's just focus on semantics and on one particular area . . ." Listening for signal phrases like these helps you quickly identify what the lecture topic will be.

Find audioscript for the other Coaching Tips at www.pearsonlongman.com/contemporarytopics.

Talk about the Topic *page 8*

Hannah: It was interesting lecture, but I have to say, I found a couple of parts confusing.

Manny: Really? Like what?

Hannah: Well, he said that language change is inevitable, right?

River: Yeah, it's like "a living thing." I guess that means all living things develop, change, you know.

Hannah: OK. And that we can't stop change from happening. Is that how everyone took it?

Mia: So far, we're with you.

Hannah: But later he seemed to say that groups choose to change language—that is, they use slang—because they want to make a statement or create their own identities.

Mia: Yeah, OK. So what's the confusion?

Hannah: Well, presumably, if they can choose to change language by using slang, that means they can

also choose *not* to use it, right? And if they can choose *not* to use it . . .

Manny: Ah . . . Then they're not changing. They're choosing not to change the language. It's a choice, you're saying. I see your point.

Hannah: Thank you. So, isn't that a contradiction?

River: No, I don't think so. What he meant was that language change will happen generally. That there'll always be events, groups, or someone out there playing with the language, creating "slang."

Mia: Right. Maybe it's because communication requires us to adapt to new conditions, so we change the language to adapt. That's the inevitable part. It's going to happen. History shows us that.

Hannah: Oh, OK.

Manny: But it isn't inevitable in any particular group, or in any particular case. You're right about that—individuals have a choice about how they speak.

River: Make sense?

Hannah: Yeah, yeah. I think I get it now. Hey, thanks guys—that was a "sweet" explanation!

Take the Unit Test

1. In what order does the speaker talk about the topic?
2. Which area of language is slang associated with?
3. In defining slang, how does the speaker describe it?
4. What does slang show?
5. What are two personal benefits of slang?
6. The semanticist Hayakawa called slang "the poetry of everyday life." What did he mean?
7. The speaker says that some people see themselves as "guardians of the language." What does he mean?
8. How does the speaker feel about slang?
9. Which of these four people would you expect to use slang most?
10. What is the lecture mainly about?

Extend the Topic *page 10*

Jacky: Hi, I'm Jacky Giopoulos and I'm in Palo Alto, California, in the heart of Silicon Valley. You know, since instant messaging technology hit the market, its popularity has spread like crazy. And with the growth of cell phone messaging, it's now estimated that around 80 million Americans IM regularly! And it's changing how we talk; it's created a slang all of its own. We're all familiar with the IM slang LOL, "laugh out loud," and TTYL, "talk to you later." But let's ask these skateboarders what other slang they use. We have Sam and Stephanie. Sam, what are some of the other expressions you use?

Sam: Well there's "JK," which means "just kidding." And I use "BBL" quite a bit, which is "be back later."

Jacky: And Stephanie, what about you?

Stephanie: Oh, I'm always using "LLS"—"love you like a sister," and "OMG," which is "oh my gosh." And "TTYLGF" is kind of fun with your female pals. It means "talk to you later, girlfriend."

Jacky: OK . . . So, can you two give some examples of IM slang that have crossed over into speech. For example, I just found out that "book" means "cool." Why, why is that?

Sam: Well, it's basically the fact that when you type the words "book" and "cool" on a cell phone type pad, you use the same keys—so, like, one can mean the other.

Stephanie: Oh, and I've got another one. When you type "1," the less than symbol, "3," and "you" on a type pad, it looks like "I heart you," in other words, "I love you." On Valentine's Day, everyone was going around saying "I less than 3 you"! It was fun.

Jacky: Hey, that's funny. That story made me "ROFL"—that's "roll on the floor laughing." And on that note, it's back to the studio . . .

ANSWER KEY

Build Your Vocabulary *pages 3–4*

B. 1. c 2. a 3. b 4. a 5. c 6. b 7. a 8. b 9. b 10. c
C. Interact with Vocabulary! 1. to 2. in 3. by
4. of 5. with 6. with 7. to 8. in 9. into 10. by

Focus Your Attention *page 5*

A. Sequence markers: First, Then, Next, And last;
Four reasons: 1. to say something about themselves: create an impression or influence someone,
2. according to the situation: where and who, 3. to fit, to feel accepted, 4. the entertainment factor—be creative with the language

Listen for Main Ideas *page 6*

B. 1. T 2. F (everyone uses slang) 3. F (helps construct people's identity) 4. F (all social groups use slang) 5. T 6. T 7. F (increase) 8. F (has become)

Listen for Details *pages 6–7*

B. 1. a 2. c 3. a 4. d 5. b 6. c 7. a 8. a 9. d
10. d

Talk about the Topic *page 8*

A. 1. River 2. Mia 3. Manny 4. River **B.** Agreeing: 4; Asking for clarification or confirmation: 1, 5; Paraphrasing: 2, 3

Review Your Notes *page 9*

Def.: Informal language associated w/ particular groups; **Who uses:** everyone; **Main function of:** to construct identity & claim membership of a group/community; **Personal benefits:** 1. makes you desirable, 2. gives you status, 3. reinforces relationships, 4. it's fun; **Major inspirations:** 1. love & romance, 2. likes & dislikes, 3. new technology; **Attitudes toward:** no longer taboo but associated w/undesirable + uneducated groups; any kind of language Δ = bad

Take the Unit Test

1. d 2. d 3. d 4. c 5. c 6. c 7. d 8. a 9. b 10. c

 **UNIT 1 TEST** COMMUNICATION STUDIES:
Slang and Language Change

 Listen to each question. Circle the letter of the correct answer.

1. a. who uses slang and why, attitudes about slang, the main inspirations for slang

    b. the main inspirations for slang, attitudes about slang, who uses slang and why

    c. attitudes about slang, who uses slang and why, the main inspirations for slang

    d. who uses slang and why, the main inspirations for slang, attitudes about slang

2. a. syntax

    b. phonology

    c. orthography

    d. semantics

3. a. as a type of impolite language

    b. as a type of language spoken by young people

    c. as a type of language spoken only by deprived groups

    d. as a type of informal language

4. a. a good understanding of language usage

    b. a desire to be young and cool

    c. a desire for membership in a group

    d. a strong dislike of tradition

5. a. It makes you desirable and youthful.

    b. It's fun and shows you're rebellious.

    c. It reinforces relationships and makes you desirable.

    d. It's fun and makes you youthful.

6. a. All users of slang are poets.

    b. You have to study slang carefully to use it correctly.

    c. Slang can be creative and entertaining.

    d. It is difficult to create new slang.

7. a. They love studying language.

    b. They are experts on language.

    c. They want to decide what is and is not slang.

    d. They want to protect the language from change.

8. a. He approves of slang as a sign of life and beauty in language.

    b. He approves of slang as a necessary part of growing up.

    c. He neither approves nor disapproves of slang but sees it as inevitable.

    d. He disapproves of slang as a bad and divisive influence on young people.

9. a. a 45-year-old school teacher

    b. a 25-year-old computer programmer

    c. a 39-year-old company director

    d. a 32-year-old linguist

10. a. why slang will never be accepted by everybody

    b. why only young people use slang

    c. how and why slang is widely used

    d. the importance of slang in academic life

UNIT OVERVIEW

In this unit, students first learn how gifted children are identified by considering issues such as natural aptitude for a skill, quality of performance, and speed of learning. Second, the students hear about a few of the personality characteristics of gifted children: their intensity, their high levels of physical and mental energy, and their idealism. Follow-up projects extend the topic to issues such as the problems associated with giftedness and the average person's potential for genius.

Connect to the Topic *page 12*   *~10 minutes*

Students take a survey about their beliefs concerning giftedness. Survey questions concern issues such as how common giftedness is and the role of natural ability.

Build Your Vocabulary *pages 13–14*   *~15 minutes*

Students study the following words and phrases related to psychology and giftedness:

alert	idealistic about	reach the conclusion
aptitude	imagination	that
aptitude for	inconsistencies	some more than
creative imagination	innate ability	others
details about	make predictions	strategy
devoted	motivation	underlying
devoted time (to)	predominant	underlying reasons
exhibit		

For the Interact with Vocabulary! activity, you may want to encourage students to first notice the boldfaced words. Figuring out these collocations can help students more quickly unscramble the sentences.

Focus Your Attention *page 15*   *~10 minutes*

Students learn cues that lecturers use when focusing on examples:

For example . . .   *An example of this is . . .*
For instance . . .   *One example would be . . .*
. . . such as . . .   *Let me give you an example of this.*

Listen to the Lecture *pages 16–17*   *~30 minutes*

Students consider how gifted children are identified (Before You Listen) before listening to the unit lecture on gifted children. Students then answer multiple-choice items (Listen for Main Ideas) and true/false items (Listen for Details).
Lecture video time: 5 min. 35 sec.   *Number of episodes: 8*

Talk about the Topic *page 18*   *~20 minutes*

Four students—Yhinny, Michael, May, and Qiang—discuss the lecture. Part A focuses on matching these students with ideas from the discussion. In Part B, your students work on these discussion strategies:

- Offering a fact or example: "Mozart, he practiced for hours! His father forced him."
- Asking for clarification or confirmation: "Like talents that we're born with?"
- Asking for opinions or ideas: "So how do I identify a gifted child?"

For Part C, students are encouraged to use the discussion strategies they've learned. They may use phrases from the student discussion or come up with their own. Keep in mind that there aren't always absolutely "correct" answers—sometimes a speaker's words are subject to interpretation. The most important point is that students support their opinions with facts and reasons. *Student discussion video time: 1 min. 38 sec.*

Review Your Notes *page 19*   *~15 minutes*

Students focus on reconstructing their notes, paying attention to main points as they explain ideas from the lecture.

BONUS ACTIVITY

As a lead-in to the unit test, you can ask students to work with a partner and list what they consider the five most important ideas from the lecture. Pairs can then share their answers and the reasons for those answers with each other.

Take the Unit Test *Teacher's Pack page 13*   *~15 minutes*

You may want to play the lecture again just before giving the test. Students answer standard test questions about the content of the lecture. Specifically, the test covers the following: the main idea of the lecture, the definition of "untrained natural abilities," how to identify a gifted child, the best predictor of giftedness, the personality characteristics of gifted children, and the speaker's attitude toward gifted children.

Extend the Topic *pages 20–21*   *~30 minutes*

- Listening and Discussion: Students listen to a podcast interview on the problems associated with giftedness, then discuss what they've heard.
- Reading and Discussion: Students read and discuss a promotion about a book promising to help readers discover and develop their own genius.
- Research and Presentation: Students conduct Internet research on someone they believe is gifted, then present their findings.

Focus Your Attention:
Try It Out! *page 15*

Speaker: OK. Now, it's important to understand that there are many kinds of special talents. For example, the ability to do math, the ability to dance, and the ability to sing are quite different from one another. In addition, some special talents, such as leadership ability, are very general because they involve such a wide range of skills. On the other hand, other talents are fairly specific and narrow. An example would be the ability to play a musical instrument well—for instance, a guitar. One more example would be the ability to do mathematics. Great talent for mathematics doesn't necessarily mean that the person has great talent in other areas . . .

Listen for Main Ideas and Listen for Details *pages 16–17*

Child psychology instructor: E1 Let me begin by asking you to think about someone you believe is exceptionally talented. Someone you were in school with or someone in your own family. OK? Have you thought of someone? Now, my question to you is, how did that person become so talented? Were they born that way? Were they a fast learner? Did they seem to love learning? Were they unusually alert and curious? My guess is that your answer to most of these questions is "yes." E2 Well, today I'd like to talk about children who are very talented, children often referred to as "gifted," and I'll talk about three points concerning this topic. First, I'll explain how these gifted children are identified. Second, I'll talk about some of the personality characteristics of these children. Third, I'll talk about how these gifted children approach learning. They have very good learning strategies that all of us can learn to use. All right. Let's move on to the first point. E3 Now, how would you identify a gifted child? Think of when you were in elementary school or high school. I'm sure that you knew some students who exhibited exceptional talents. Maybe they were particularly good at sports, mathematics, or art. They were easy to notice, right? Well, see if these ideas make sense to you. First, giftedness is partly the result of untrained natural abilities. You could call this "an aptitude" for something. So when we see a very young child who shows above-average athletic ability, for example, we often conclude that the child has an innate ability for sports. E4 Now, I just said "above-average ability," and that's a second thing that we notice: the quality. The child's performance is special because it's surprisingly good, particularly when we consider the child's age. For instance, a six-year-old who could play Mozart's Sonata in D Major would be considered gifted. The third way we can identify children is by the speed at which they learn. They generally learn faster, make fewer mistakes, make the same mistake fewer times, and need less practice than other children. Some psychologists believe that this third point, speed of learning, is perhaps the best indicator that a child has special abilities. E5 Now, I'd like to highlight some personality characteristics of gifted children. Of course, gifted children have many types of personalities, so what I'm going to describe here are characteristics that are often, but not always, found in gifted children. For one, gifted children are often very intense. When they do something, especially something they enjoy, they devote all their energy and determination to it. They can concentrate for a very long time. Secondly, they tend to have high energy levels. When they are young, they are constantly moving, and this degree of physical energy is often matched by a similar amount of mental and emotional energy. Their minds are always in motion, always thinking, always looking for the next interesting puzzle to solve. A final predominant characteristic is that they are often idealistic about the world, the people they know, and their environment. They can be perfectionists, especially where their own work is concerned. E6 OK, now let's look at some of the ways that gifted children approach learning something, practical strategies that you and I can try. The first approach is related to motivation. Gifted children appear to be intensely curious about any and every topic. They typically don't care whether the knowledge or skill is useful or not. A second trait is that they are observant and they notice many details about things. This allows them to thoroughly understand whatever they are studying and to notice any inconsistencies. E7 Finally, they want to know the inner workings of things, so they are very interested in causes and effects. In other words, they want to know the underlying principles and use those principles for making generalizations and predictions about the thing they are studying. I might also add here that they enjoy using their imagination. E8 Now, let's pause a moment to think of what I've just said here about approaches to learning. Gifted children are motivated, they are alert and observant, they concentrate intensely, they try to understand cause-and-effect relationships, and they make an effort to think creatively. How well could you and I learn to do something if we approached it like I've just described? My guess is that we could do pretty well.

Coaching Tips

[1] Listening: Identifying topics through questions
The speaker asks a series of questions about your thoughts concerning gifted people. How can answering these questions help prepare you for the rest of the lecture? As you think about your own answers, you're mentally readying yourself for the lecture. In other words, the speaker has given you an outline of the lecture in the form of questions.

Find audioscript for the other Coaching Tips at www.pearsonlongman.com/contemporarytopics.

Talk about the Topic *page 18*

Michael: You know, the lecture actually reminded me of this idea called the "10,000 hour, ten-year rule." Has anyone else heard of it?

May: Huh-uh.

Qiang: No.

Yhinny: Oh yeah, I have, I have. It says something like you have to study something or practice something really hard for either 10,000 hours or ten years to become really great at something.

May: Whoa, well, that's encouraging. That means that I just have to study English for another five years to be really good at it?

Qiang: Well, I have to say, I found it a little surprising that the instructor really didn't talk about—or she didn't really emphasize—that's the importance of innate talents more.

May: Like, talents that we're born with? I don't know, for like music and literature, art, science.

Qiang: Yeah.

Yhinny: I think she actually did cover that, in a way. I think she just wanted to stress the parts of genius that we can control. Kind of like being motivated, being curious or creative when you approach something.

Qiang: OK. But you have to acknowledge the innate part is a huge factor. I mean, look at Mozart and his innate talent for music. Or Emily Dickinson and her innate talent for literature. You think anyone can do what they did just by being curious or practicing a lot?

May: No, you're right, they had talents, but they built on them. I mean, Mozart, he practiced for hours. His father forced him.

Qiang: So, he was born with talent, but he had to work really hard to develop it.

May: Yeah.

Michael: Well, speaking of working hard, maybe we should get back into our notes? All right, so how to identify a gifted child?

Take the Unit Test

1. What is the main idea of the lecture?
2. Which of the following topics does the speaker *not* talk about?
3. What is meant by "untrained natural abilities"?
4. What is one way to identify a gifted child?
5. Which of the following can we infer about giftedness?
6. What is the best indicator of giftedness?
7. Which of the following is probably true about gifted children?
8. Why are gifted children often able to notice inconsistencies?
9. Why do some gifted children want to understand cause-and-effect relationships?
10. What is the speaker's attitude toward gifted children?

Extend the Topic *page 20*

John: So I think that we can appreciate how truly special these children are. But I have to ask you whether the situation is as positive as it sounds so far. I mean, aren't there some drawbacks to being gifted?

Dr. Andrews: Well, yes, John, there are. For instance, the high energy levels that many gifted children have are extremely difficult for many parents to deal with day in and day out. I've talked to quite a few parents who are simply exhausted as they try to meet the demands of their gifted child.

John: I can imagine how hard that could be. You also mentioned that some gifted children are perfectionists. Does that cause trouble for either the child or others around them?

Dr. Andrews: Absolutely, John. Although perfectionist tendencies can drive gifted children to greatness, they can also place a great deal of stress and pressure on the child—as well as on friends and family.

John: Exactly why are people around the child affected?

Dr. Andrews: It's because the child can become quite critical of others.

John: Oh, I see. The child expects others to be perfect also.

Dr. Andrews: That's right. So while having a gifted child is wonderful in some ways, it can be quite challenging in others. . . .

ANSWER KEY

Build Your Vocabulary *pages 13–14*

A. 1. c 2. c 3. c 4. a 5. b 6. a 7. c 8. a 9. c 10. b
B. Interact with Vocabulary! 1. reach the conclusion that a child is gifted 2. aptitude for dance became apparent 3. I understand the underlying reasons for 4. an innate ability for doing mathematics 5. because of her unusually creative imagination 6. has devoted a lot of time 7. somewhat idealistic about the people 8. they notice many details about 9. they can make predictions about 10. some strategies are more effective than others

Focus Your Attention *page 15*

A. Phrases: For example, such as, An example would be, for instance, One more example would be; **Examples:** the ability to do math, dance, sing; leadership ability; the ability to play a musical instrument well; the ability to do mathematics

Listen for Main Ideas *pages 16–17*

B. 1. c 2. a 3. b 4. a 5. b 6. b

Listen for Details *page 17*

B. 1. T 2. F (fewer mistakes) 3. F (no difficulty) 4. F (and high levels of emotional energy) 5. T 6. T 7. T

Talk about the Topic *page 18*

A. 1. Qiang 2. Qiang, May 3. May **B.** Offering a fact or example: 1, 3, 4; Asking for clarification or confirmation: 2; Asking for opinions or ideas: 5

Review Your Notes *page 19*

3 ways to identify: 1. untrained natural ability, 2. above-average ability/quality of the performance, 3. the speed of learning; **3 personality characteristics:** 1. very intense, 2. high energy levels, 3. idealistic; **3 learning strategies:** 1. intensely curious, 2. observant, 3. interested in the inner workings/causes and effects

Take the Unit Test

1. c 2. d 3. b 4. b 5. d 6. b 7. a 8. c 9. d 10. c

UNIT 2 TEST CHILD PSYCHOLOGY: The Genius Within

Listen to each question. Circle the letter of the correct answer.

1. a. the successes that gifted children enjoy
   b. children with exceptional musical talent
   c. the characteristics of gifted children
   d. the challenges that gifted children face

2. a. how gifted children are identified
   b. the personality characteristics of gifted children
   c. how gifted children approach learning
   d. how successful gifted children are as adults

3. a. a good education
   b. an aptitude for doing something
   c. large amounts of practice
   d. a strong desire to do something

4. a. The child is constantly moving.
   b. The child's performance is surprisingly good.
   c. The child is very friendly.
   d. The child has a good sense of humor.

5. a. Gifted children are quite similar to one another.
   b. The brothers and sisters of gifted children are probably gifted themselves.
   c. The parents of gifted children are also gifted.
   d. Giftedness comes in many forms and can involve many different skills.

6. a. a positive personality
   b. speed of learning
   c. musical ability
   d. an outgoing personality

7. a. They are highly motivated to learn.
   b. They are bored in regular classrooms.
   c. They usually do not enjoy playing sports.
   d. They are almost always cheerful.

8. a. because they are concerned about what others think
   b. because they read about many topics
   c. because they are very observant and notice details
   d. because they practice more than other children

9. a. because they hate to make mistakes
   b. because they are highly motivated
   c. because they want to see others' reactions
   d. because they want to make generalizations and predictions

10. a. She disapproves of classifying children in different ways.
    b. She is skeptical about their abilities.
    c. She regards them very positively.
    d. She appears uninterested in them.

TEACHING TIPS

UNIT OVERVIEW

In this unit, students consider the importance most people in society place on status and the various ways in which such social status is indicated. The lecture focuses in particular on the relationship between success, status, and power, and the ways in which people show their status (status symbols) including fashion, "trophy kids," and status skills. Follow-up activities look at the link between social status and lifespan as well as different kinds of "status lifestyles."

Connect to the Topic *page 22*   *~10 minutes*

As a warm-up activity, consider asking students to read the cartoon and discuss what's funny about it. In the survey, students rank indicators of social status from strongest to weakest. Try to encourage students to talk about why they have rated the indicators in the order they have. This should make for an interesting discussion and produce some rich ideas and language.

Build Your Vocabulary *pages 23–24*   *~15 minutes*

Students study the following words and phrases related to sociology and social status:

advertise	global	regardless of
affluent	hierarchies	relates to
attaining	iconic	show off
concentrate on	in recognition of	signified by
consensus of opinion	income	status symbols
consumption	indicator of	work your way up
depends on	reflecting	

After the Interact with Vocabulary! activity, you may want to have students practice using the boldfaced words with their partners.

Focus Your Attention *page 25*   *~10 minutes*

Students learn cues that help them to identify key terms and definitions during lectures:

Lecturer cues:	Introductory phrases:
repeating	*There is (one key concept) . . .*
spelling	*One (example) is . . .*
pausing	*The first (theory) is . . .*
slowing down	*Let's look at (this idea of) . . .*
speaking more loudly	
asking for confirmation of understanding	

Listen to the Lecture *pages 26–27*   *~30 minutes*

Students consider ways that people show their social status (Before You Listen) before listening to the unit lecture on social status. Students then answer true/false items (Listen for Main Ideas) and fill in sentence blanks with correct words or phrases (Listen for Details).
Lecture video time: 6 min. 38 sec.   *Number of episodes: 7*

Talk about the Topic *page 28*   *~20 minutes*

Four students—Ayman, Molly, Rob, and Alana—discuss the lecture. Part A focuses on matching these students with examples from the discussion. In Part B, your students work on these discussion strategies:

- Asking for opinions or ideas: "Can anyone give some examples of some 'conspicuous consumption' that they've seen?"
- Paraphrasing: "So the car was his status symbol."
- Keeping the discussion on topic: "Hey, can we please focus on the lecture?"

For Part C, students are encouraged to use the discussion strategies they've learned. They may use phrases from the student discussion and/or the Discussion Strategy box, or come up with their own.
Student discussion video time: 1 min. 33 sec.

Review Your Notes *page 29*   *~15 minutes*

Students focus on reconstructing their notes, paying attention to key terms and definitions.

BONUS ACTIVITY

You can divide the class into two groups and give them a quiz on the key terms of the lecture. Alternatively, they can quiz each other. They can either ask what a key term means or provide a definition and request the term it is defining.

Take the Unit Test *Teacher's Pack page 19*   *~15 minutes*

You may want to play the lecture again just before giving the test. Students answer standard test questions about the content of the lecture. Specifically, the test covers the following: the order in which ideas are presented, relationships between concepts, expressions the lecturer uses, a definition of conspicuous consumption, trophy wives and husbands, status skills, storytelling, and the main idea of the lecture.

Extend the Topic *pages 30–31*   *~30 minutes*

- Listening and Discussion: Students listen to and discuss a documentary trailer about research on the link between social status and longevity.
- Reading and Discussion: Students read about and discuss transient lifestyles.
- Research and Presentation: Students conduct additional research on a status lifestyle and present to their classmates.

Focus Your Attention:
Try It Out! *page 25*

Speaker: There are a few societies around the world where everyone has equal status. In the great majority of societies, though, there exists some kind of social hierarchy, sometimes referred to as *social stratification*. That's *social stratification*: s-t-r-a-t-i-f-i-c-a-t-i-o-n. Got that? This stratification means that those occupying high status have more power and privilege than others. Their opinions, ways of thinking, values, needs, and feelings are thought to have more value. This situation can lead to what's called *status conflict*, where people lower down the hierarchy feel that the inequality has become too great. That they have too little recognition, worth, or authority, and too small a share in resources. Essentially, this is a reaction to a kind of injustice and discrimination in favor of the *status quo*, which is the existing situation. In other words, those who are lower in the hierarchy want change, and may be prepared to fight for their own values. . . .

Listen for Main Ideas and Listen for Details *pages 26–27*

Sociology lecturer: **E1** Let's continue our discussion of social hierarchies by talking about how people achieve status in society, and how they try to show it off. Now, whether we like it or not, our status in society depends on things like class, education, wealth, and recognition of success. And it is society who forms a general consensus of what these things signify, what value they have. Of course, some elements of our status, such as social class, we can't control, although it's sometimes possible to work your way up the social pecking order. Other aspects of our status, like wealth and professional success, we *can* control, at least to some degree. And it's these elements, those which we can control, that I'd like to concentrate on today. **E2** Let's look first at the concept of success as it relates to establishing our social status. In most societies, the bottom line is that people generally want to be associated with success. Why? Because it makes them valued in society, and it gives them power, influence, and prestige. So what's the quickest way to get this power, do you think? Through attaining wealth, of course, the one thing within everyone's grasp, regardless of their roots. **E3** Now, because wealth and success are so important to people, so too are the symbols that signify those things. These so-called "status symbols," usually possessions or activities, are the things we use to measure a person's social or economic prestige. But, for social or economic prestige to be measured, it needs to be noticed, right? Which brings me to conspicuous consumption—the different ways we consume in order to show people our wealth, and not because we really need the things we buy. You see, we don't just want to be affluent and successful, we want others to know we're affluent and successful. And status symbols allow us to advertise our success. We're all familiar with the big house in the exclusive residential district with the expensive BMW parked in the driveway, right? Conspicuous consumption is about showing off our wealth and success. **E4** So, let's now look at how we do this. Through what symbols do we try to show our status? Well, there's fashion, for a start. The idea of using clothes to signal social status has a long history. However, while in the past status was indicated by who was permitted to wear what, today it's indicated by the cost of a person's clothing, which, of course, is why designer labels have assumed almost iconic status in global twenty-first century culture, a trend originating largely in the fashion houses of Europe around a century ago. The idea is, if you can afford Dior, Chanel, or Vivienne Westwood, then you must be a high flyer. **E5** OK, how many of you have heard of "trophy wives" or "trophy husbands"? Anyone? How we sort of acquire husbands or wives like we acquire trophies, to act as symbols of status. Well, it seems that "trophy kids" are the new indicators of social status, offspring who say something about their parents. Let's have a look at this idea now. You know, if you look back at census data over recent decades, richer has tended to mean fewer kids. As the average incomes of families have increased, the smaller those families have become. This is changing though, and recent data suggests that the better off you are, the more kids you'll have. Why this change? Because, like I said, kids are a great way of signaling status. Perhaps they go to the most prestigious schools, enjoy elite sports, and so on. Their parents may be able to talk about the yachting or horse-riding championships their children have won, or perhaps their entry into Harvard or Yale. The point? These kids are symbols to the outside world that their parents have made it. **E6** Now, as we've seen, status symbols have a lot to do with ownership and the idea of conspicuous consumption, being able to show off your wealth. But there's a new idea now being talked about called "status skills," the idea that by mastering certain skills, we acquire status. TV shows are reflecting—and probably driving—this new obsession, and more and more organizations are jumping on the bandwagon here. They're trying to meet demand by offering professionally run courses in areas such as cooking, dancing, gardening, wine-making, scuba-diving. And vacations are increasingly selling on the basis of "skills rather than thrills," with companies building in opportunities to develop often exotic or traditionally elite skills, such as horse-riding, parachuting, bungee jumping, and other fun stuff like that. E7 Now, acquiring these skills is one thing; however, their value as status symbols is only realized through what's called "storytelling." In other words, through showing off what you've learned by talking about it, through creating opportunities for those you want to impress or influence to see your skills. That's what brings the status!

Coaching Tips

[1] **Note-taking: Organizing main ideas** Did you hear the main ideas? Did you write them in your notes? There were two. Remember, it's a good idea to begin your note-taking by writing down what the speaker will cover and leaving lots of space between the points so that you can add details about each. Your notes might look like this: [see video for note-taking example].

Find audioscript for the other Coaching Tips at www.pearsonlongman.com/contemporarytopics.

Talk about the Topic *page 28*

Molly: So, based on the lecture, I guess you could say I've got status—check out my designer purse.

Ayman: No, Molly. It's imitation status, since your bag's a total knock-off.

Alana: Oh. Who cares? It's gorgeous! Where did you get it?

Rob: Oh no, no. Hey, can we please focus on the lecture? All right, we have a lot to review. So all right, here's one key idea: conspicuous consumption. Can anyone give some examples of some conspicuous consumption that they've seen?

Molly: Yeah. A couple summers ago I worked for a family in Chicago as a nanny. And they had this brand new bright red Mercedes Benz, and the husband would wash it in the driveway like every single weekend.

Ayman: Well at least he did it himself.

Molly: No, no. That's not my point. My point is that he wanted everyone to see that it was his, so he'd polish it for like an hour.

Rob: So the car was his status symbol.

Molly: Exactly. I have another example, too, which is a little bit different. So, I went to this wedding reception last June; it was friends of my sisters, and it was this beautiful outdoor event. But they just served us so much food, like steak and lobster, chocolate torte and Italian sorbet.

Rob: I am so jealous of you.

Molly: No, it was gross. Because it was more food than any person could possibly eat, you know? And it just all went to waste—it was just dumped straight into the garbage.

Ayman: So you're saying they were trying to show their guests how wealthy they were, right?

Molly: Exactly.

Ayman: Oh.

Molly: And you don't even want to ask how much the bride's dress cost.

Rob: No, we don't. So . . .

Alana: OK.

Take the Unit Test

1. In what order does the speaker talk about the topic of social status?
2. Which element of social status are we unable to control?
3. What is the relationship between success and power?
4. The speaker says that wealth is "within everyone's grasp." What does he mean?
5. What is the best definition of "conspicuous consumption"?
6. What does the speaker see "trophy wives" and "trophy husbands" as?
7. Which situation best describes American families?
8. Which of these is probably a status skill?
9. Which of these illustrates storytelling?
10. What is the main idea of the lecture?

Extend the Topic *page 30*

Martin: Dr. Boyle, why do scientists think that there might be a connection between social status and lifespan? ✓ video ?

Dr. Boyle: Monkeys, Martin. Like us, monkeys live in very hierarchical societies, and researchers have found a strong link between their position in the hierarchy and their health. Those further up the hierarchy are generally healthier—and therefore live longer.

Martin: And research has indicated the same for human societies?

Dr. Boyle: That's right. A major study of government employees, for instance, found that those lower down the pecking order—the clerks, messengers, and so on—were much more likely to suffer heart disease than those at the top.

Martin: Is there a direct relationship between health and status? I mean, is a person with a lot of status a lot healthier?

Dr. Boyle: Yes, that seems to be the case. And even a small difference in status can have a pretty major impact on health. For example, would you believe that people with doctorate degrees live longer than those with masters degrees?

Martin: Whoa, really?

Dr. Boyle: Really. Or that individuals who are awarded Nobel Prizes live longer than those who are merely nominated? One-point-four years longer, to be precise. And that gap increases by another eight months when the comparison is between winners and nominees from the same country.

Martin: Huh. So, presumably, the prize money they won was the reason for the better health and longer life. Right?

Dr. Boyle: You'd think so, wouldn't you? But, apparently, the winning made the difference, not the money, research has found.

Martin: Fascinating stuff! But why? Have researchers gotten to the bottom of this? . . .

ANSWER KEY

✓ Build Your Vocabulary *pages 23–24*

A. 1. product; public's attention 2. plenty; money; possessions 3. reaching; something 4. buying; products 5. affecting; world 6. systems; lower 7. famous; representing; idea 8. money; generates 9. indicating; situation; idea 10. own; indicate; successful **D. Interact with Vocabulary!** 1. on 2. of 3. on 4. of 5. of 6. of 7. to 8. off 9. by 10. up

Focus Your Attention *page 25*

A. *stratification* (those occupying high status have more power and privilege than others; their thinking/values/needs/feelings have more value); *status conflict* (where people lower down the hierarchy feel the inequality has become too great; a reaction to injustice/discrimination); *status quo* (the existing situation)

Listen for Main Ideas *page 26*

B. 1. T 2. T 3. T 4. F (still signal status through cost) 5. F (are becoming) 6. F (is connected/you can show off your skills)

Listen for Details *page 27*

B. 1. education 2. social class 3. Success 4. Wealth 5. Europe 6. twentieth 7. parents 8. Television programs 9. Dancing; gardening 10. impress; influence

Talk about the Topic *page 28*

A. 1. Ayman, Molly, Alana 2. Ayman, Molly, Rob 3. Ayman, Molly, Rob **B.** Asking for opinions or ideas: 2; Paraphrasing: 3, 4; Keeping the discussion on topic: 1

Review Your Notes *page 29*

Social hierarchies: groups w/ dif't status w/in societies; *Success and social status:* your position in society & how it's perceived; *Status symbols:* things that signify wealth & success; *Conspicuous consumption:* the ways we consume in order to show people our $$$; *Designer labels:* labels that indicate the names of $$$ designers; *Trophy kids:* offspring who signal their parents' status; *Status skills:* activities that bring status; *Storytelling:* talking about your skills in order to acquire status

Take the Unit Test

1. a 2. c 3. c 4. b 5. d 6. b 7. b 8. c 9. c 10. d

Extend the Topic *page 30*

A. 1. because they live in hierarchical societies like us

UNIT 3 TEST SOCIOLOGY: Social Status: Flaunting Your Success

 Listen to each question. Circle the letter of the correct answer.

1. a. power and success, status symbols, status skills
   b. status skills, power and success, status symbols
   c. status skills, status symbols, power and success
   d. status symbols, power and success, status skills

2. a. wealth
   b. education
   c. social class
   d. professional success

3. a. The more power you have, the more success you have.
   b. The more power you have, the less success you have.
   c. The more success you have, the more power you have.
   d. The more success you have, the less power you have.

4. a. It's easy to obtain wealth.
   b. It's possible for anybody to become wealthy.
   c. Everybody desires to be wealthy.
   d. A desire for wealth is part of human nature.

5. a. consuming things in order to have a wealthy lifestyle
   b. buying goods that show social class
   c. purchasing products in front of lots of people
   d. consuming selectively in order to demonstrate wealth

6. a. symbols of conspicuous consumption
   b. being replaced by "trophy kids" as indicators of social status
   c. rewards for being successful
   d. the parents of "trophy kids"

7. a. Wealthier families have become smaller in recent years.
   b. Wealthier families have become larger in recent years.
   c. American families have remained almost unchanged.
   d. The gap between rich and poor families has decreased.

8. a. playing soccer
   b. writing poetry
   c. sailing
   d. driving

9. a. telling someone about a recent vacation you took to a private island
   b. showing off your expensive new car to neighbors
   c. telling about and serving friends a dish you learned to make in an Italian cooking class
   d. hiring someone to cut your lawn

10. a. It's impossible to change our social status.
    b. Wealth and status are not closely linked.
    c. Indicators of social status often change.
    d. Social status is about possessing what others don't.

BUSINESS: The Art of Marketing in a Global Culture

TEACHING TIPS

UNIT OVERVIEW

This unit introduces students to the subject of the "global village" and the idea that as the world becomes increasingly interconnected, cultures are becoming more homogeneous. It looks in particular at some of the causes of this phenomenon, as well as the implications for businesses seeking to market their products internationally.

Connect to the Topic   *page 32*   *~10 minutes*

Students take a product survey. The survey is designed to assess whether certain products (and their advertising slogans and/or logos) are widely recognized, owned, and desired by students. You may want to clarify that students should first fill in the Product and Slogan/Logo columns, then complete the other three columns by asking classmates the questions. This activity lends itself particularly well to multicultural classes but can also be effective in monocultural groups. Have students discuss the significance of their findings as a class.

Build Your Vocabulary   *pages 33–34*   *~15 minutes*

Students study the following words and phrases related to business and global marketing:

accustomed to	emphasis on	ideological
appeals to	enables	implication of
consult on	enticed by	media
converge	entire	promote
cooperation between	guaranteed	universal
element of risk	homogeneous	verbal

After the Interact with Vocabulary! activity, you may want to have students practice using the boldfaced words with their partners. Knowing collocations can help students expand their vocabularies and increase their fluency.

Focus Your Attention   *page 35*   *~10 minutes*

Students learn symbols and abbreviations to make them more efficient note-takers:

Symbols:

=	equals; is the same as	]	excludes
≠	does not equal/is not the same as	+ or &	and; also
>	is more than/larger than	...	continues; and so on
<	is less than/smaller than	$	dollars
∴	therefore; as a result/because	%	percent
↑	to increase	#	number
↓	to decrease	~	for example or
→	leads to; causes		approximately
←	is caused by; depends on	Δ	change
[	includes	k	thousand

Abbreviations:

ad	advertisement		*ex* or *e.g.*	example
av	average		*fb*	feedback
co	company		*glob*	globalization
cult diff	cultural difference		*intl*	international
def	definition		*Prof MS*	Professor Michael Stevens

Try to elicit students' own suggestions for symbols and abbreviations, and emphasize the essentially personal nature of how we shorten information.

Listen to the Lecture *pages 36–37*   *~30 minutes*

Students consider causes and consequences of globalization (Before You Listen) before listening to the unit lecture on marketing in a global culture. Students then select the correct words based on information provided by the lecturer (Listen for Main Ideas). Next they answer a series of true/false items (Listen for Details).
Lecture video time: 6 min. 36 sec.   Number of episodes: 8

Talk about the Topic *page 38*   *~20 minutes*

Four students—Michael, Yhinny, Qiang, and May—discuss the lecture. Part A focuses on matching these students with comments from the discussion. In Part B, your students work on these discussion strategies:

- Expressing an opinion: "We're so similar in terms of the 'stuff' that we have."
- Disagreeing: "I don't know. I think most modern cultures are similar, like Japan, Korea, the U.S., and the U.K."
- Offering a fact or example: "Like, we all listen to the same musicians."

For Part C, students are encouraged to use the discussion strategies they've learned. They may use phrases from the student discussion and/or the Discussion Strategy box, or come up with their own.
Student discussion video time: 1 min. 15 sec.

Review Your Notes *page 39*   *~15 minutes*

Students focus on reconstructing their notes. Encourage them to use symbols and abbreviations where possible.

Take the Unit Test *Teacher's Pack page 25*   *~15 minutes*

You may want to play the lecture again just before giving the test. Students answer standard test questions about the content of the lecture. Specifically, the test covers the following: causes of globalization, the notion of universal appeal, the media as a marketing tool, the lecturer's feelings, definitions of *global* and *local*, definitions of high-/low-context cultures, the main idea of the lecture, and marketing failures.

Extend the Topic *pages 40–41*   *~30 minutes*

- Listening and Discussion: Students listen to an interview about promotional and preventative messages in advertising, then discuss.
- Reading and Discussion: Students read about four dimensions used to describe cultural behavior, then discuss in pairs.
- Research and Presentation: Students research an advertisement in preparation for a class presentation.

Focus Your Attention:
Try It Out! *page 35*

Speaker: Now, it's estimated that e-mail marketing spending will reach $1.1 billion by 2010. In that time, B2C spending—business-to-consumer spending—will increase by 5 percent annually, to $897 million. And B2B spending— that is, business-to-business spending—will increase by 2.4 percent annually to $206 million. So there's a lot of money invested in e-mail marketing, and that reflects the importance companies place on it. After all, it reaches international as well as national markets and is quite cost effective. In fact, it's estimated that 80 percent of retailers use regular customer e-mails to build customer relationships. But how effective is e-mail marketing? Well, it depends on whose statistics you use. One organization claims that of 44.4 million messages sent, 95.6 percent were delivered. However, only 28.9 percent were actually opened. Apparently, making simple changes can increase success rates by more than 50 percent. For example, increasing the number of images and making the layout style more attractive. Also, business-to-business e-mails are more effective if the company or brand name is in the subject line. . . .

Listen for Main Ideas and Listen for Details *pages 36–37*

Business lecturer: E1 I now want to look at an increasingly important aspect of international marketing: globalization. Globalization is the idea that as international travel and communication expand, the world's becoming more homogeneous. Different cultures are converging as people everywhere become increasingly similar in the way they live. There are the fads and fashions people follow, the products they buy, how they relax, the heroes they look up to, and so on. So as we travel around the world, we've become accustomed to seeing the familiar: cyber cafes, CDs of bands we love, Starbucks coffee houses, advertisements for well-known brands. In fact, I bet you can think of plenty of other examples. Think: Google, cell phones, MTV, the familiar faces of top fashion models and sporting icons, right? Let's consider, then, first some of the causes of globalization. Then let's think about its implications for businesses looking to market their products globally. E2 First then, the causes of globalization. Clearly, flight has been a key factor here, perhaps *the* key factor, and as its popularity has increased so has its affordability. Today, most people travel by air. For those traveling to holiday destinations it's the preferred way to go. It allows us to go further quicker. And for business people, it enables them to do business face-to-face on the other side of the world and reduces time away from the office. The resulting interaction between cultures has surely promoted shared values and attitudes. This is an important feature of globalization. E3 Then there's the news and entertainment industry. We can't really talk about global culture without considering the huge influence of the Internet, TV, radio, newspapers, magazines, and film. Today, these are multi-million-dollar industries, and most films, documentaries, quiz shows, and soap operas are made in the hope that they'll be bought and shown around the world. Many eventually become powerful and lucrative international brands. Popular TV series are watched on every continent and have near-universal appeal. Why? Well, because they're based on common human experiences. They evoke feelings and emotions we all share. E4 And this brings me to a key element of the news and entertainment industry and its role in helping create a global society: advertising. Ads are a common feature of television, magazines, and, of course, Internet sites. Don't you just hate those pop-up windows? Advertising works through the media, driving fads and fashions. So this makes the media a potent marketing tool, see? Because it spreads ideas incredibly widely, quickly, and effectively. E5 The third and final cause of globalization I want to highlight is politics. I want you to think specifically about the dissolution of social and economic barriers through political activity and international agreements. Take the European Union, for example. Here, a group of countries with quite different and distinctive cultures and traditions have come together in the spirit of cooperation. Many Europeans now have begun to feel that they're members of a larger, pan-European culture. Increasingly, heads of government—and not just in the EU—appear to be consulting and acting in unison on issues affecting the entire world. Issues like the environment, crime, world poverty, etcetera. Arguably, these things are lessening ideological differences between nations. And because they're reported on news channels like CNN and seen by millions, they help create a sense of pulling in the same direction. They create a feeling that there's a common culture of humanity, if you like. E6 Now, these phenomena have created easier access to global markets, no doubt. But marketing success, as measured by sales figures, is not guaranteed. And this brings me to the second part of my lecture: the implications of globalization for marketing. You know, although different markets may share common human wants and needs, marketing successfully to those wants and needs is never universal. Marketing professionals must be mindful of the local culture's values and buying behaviors when deciding strategy. This distinction between global and local culture is sometimes referred to in terms of the *universal* and the *particular*, respectively. A product becomes a universal icon only because it has particular appeal to many individual cultures across the globe. It's the job of a company's regional manager to ensure that the product has local appeal. E7 Another challenge in marketing messages across cultures is understanding differing communication styles. Anthropologists make a distinction between high-context and low-context cultures. In high-context cultures—Asian and Hispanic cultures, for instance—communication depends heavily on context. This means the nonverbal aspects of communication. In low-context cultures—like the U.S., for example—communication is more explicit and verbal. So, an example. In Japan, an ad promoting a luxury car might contain very little dialogue but a lot of impressive scenery, sophisticated gadgetry, and stirring music. These elements rely on the power of association. In contrast, in America, the ad's emphasis might be on a spoken message explaining the technology behind the car. Something more explicit. E8 Now, as a lesson in what not to do. Let's take a look at two examples of companies goofing up in their efforts to market their products internationally. A company tried introducing its instant coffee to France, a country where the casual image of the product didn't fit into the French practice of preparing "real" coffee, which is a fixed part of the French morning routine. Then there's Campbell Soups which lost $30,000 in advertising in Europe before realizing that British consumers weren't familiar with the concept of condensed soup. This particular case highlights how easily marketing departments can fall into the trap of assuming that just because two countries share a language and cultural heritage, they'll be enticed by the same message. This can be a costly miscalculation.

Coaching Tips

[1] **Note-taking: Using abbreviations** The speaker uses the words *globalization* and *marketing* several times. These and other long words can be difficult to write quickly during a lecture. Using abbreviations can help you record them faster. One way to abbreviate words is to use the first several letters of the word or the first few consonants. The first time, you may want to write the full word next to your abbreviation. This will help you remember what your abbreviation means. Here are some examples of abbreviated words, taken from the introduction. [See video for note-taking example.]

Find audioscript for the other Coaching Tips at www.pearsonlongman.com/contemporarytopics.

Talk about the Topic *page 38*

May: Talk about globalization! Look at us!

Michael: Oh, you mean, all these things we've got?

May: Right. We're all from different places, but we're so similar in terms of the "stuff" that we have.

Michael: I guess that's the concept of "homogenization" he was talking about!

Yhinny: Not only the things we buy, but also the music we all know. Like, we all listen to the same musicians.

Qiang: Even so, we're still pretty different culturally. And that's an important concept for business, right?

Michael: Uh-huh.

Yhinny: Uh-huh.

Qiang: Like he said in the lecture, a lot of things are universal icons. But do they have local appeal?

Yhinny: I don't know. I think most modern cultures are similar, like Japan, Korea, the U.S., the U.K. I think most modern societies are starting to want the same things.

Michael: Yeah.

May: Like, say, McDonald's. It's become popular in so many places, even in Jordan where I'm from, mainly because it promotes such fast-paced living.

Michael: Hey, wouldn't it be cool to do research for a global marketing firm? I mean, you'd get to travel all around the world studying local people's tastes and behaviors.

May: That would be so much fun. I love to travel. It would be like a permanent vacation!

Michael: Yeah.

Take the Unit Test

1. What does the speaker suggest is the main cause of globalization?
2. Which of the following topics *doesn't* the speaker address?
3. Why do many TV series have near-universal appeal?
4. How does the speaker feel about pop-up windows on Internet sites?
5. Why is the media a powerful marketing tool?
6. Why does the speaker mention that nations' governments are acting in unison on certain issues?
7. How are the terms *global* and *local* sometimes each described?
8. What are the terms *high-context* and *low-context* used to describe?
9. What does the case of Campbell Soups illustrate?
10. What is the lecture mainly about?

Extend the Topic *page 40*

Journalist: One question I frequently find myself asking marketing professionals is, "When does culture influence consumer purchasing decisions?"

Researcher: That's a tough question, and one we've researched pretty thoroughly.

Journalist: And?

Researcher: Well, it seems that culture-based differences show up when information is processed quickly—spontaneously. If, for instance, you pass a roadside billboard, chances are you'll be influenced by advertising that appeals to your particular culture. However, if you have time to think about information more—say looking at a website—then cultural factors play a much smaller role.

Journalist: Interesting. . . . So how did you conduct your research?

Researcher: Well, we asked some American and Asian students to give their reactions to advertisements for a brand of juice. Half of the ads promoted the benefits of drinking the juice. The other half positioned juice as a preventative—as something you could drink in order to avoid health problems.

Journalist: And the results?

Researcher: Well, they were very informative. When giving their immediate reactions to the ads, the Asians preferred the preventative message—the ad that portrayed the juice as helpful in avoiding health problems. Meanwhile, the Americans preferred the promotional message—the benefits of juice. In contrast, when both groups had time to think about the message, they had the same reactions to the two ads.

Journalist: So why the difference in their immediate reactions?

Researcher: Well, it seems that Americans focus on the positive effects of purchasing decisions because they value achievement and independent thinking. Asians, on the other hand, focus on the negative consequences of their purchasing decisions. This is because they value protection and security, and have more interdependent ways of viewing the world. So, it really is culturally based . . .

ANSWER KEY

Build Your Vocabulary *pages 33–34*

B. 1. a 2. b 3. c 4. b 5. a 6. a 7. a 8. a 9. a 10. a
C. Interact with Vocabulary! 1. to 2. on 3. between 4. of 5. on 6. to 7. by 8. of

Focus Your Attention *page 35*

A. *Possible symobls used:* 2010 – e-mail marketing = $1.1 B; B2C spending ↑ 5%/yr to $897M; B2B spending ↑ 2.4%/yr to $206M; e-mail marketing = v. cost effective; ~80% use; 44.4M messages: 95.6% delivered, 28.9% opened; 50%↑; Co.; B2B

Listen for Main Ideas *pages 36–37*

B. 1. b 2. a 3. b 4. a 5. c 6. c 7. a

Listen for Details *page 37*

B. 1. F (more homogeneous) 2. F (cultural convergence) 3. F (less time) 4. T 5. F (with audiences around the world) 6. T 7. F (Advertising drives fads and fashions.) 8. F (because of political activity/int'l agreements) 9. T 10. F (more directly . . .)

Talk about the Topic *page 38*

A. 1. Michael, Yhinny 2. Michael, Yhinny 3. Michael 4. May **Note:** Since the person who makes the statement (1. May; 2. Qiang; 3. Yhinny; 4. Michael) "agrees" with it, students could argue for marking that name as well. **B.** 1. Expressing an opinion: 4; Disagreeing: 3, 4; Offering a fact or example: 1, 2

Review Your Notes *page 39*

1. World becomes more homogeneous as cultures converge; **2.** Fads & fashions, products, how people relax, heroes they look up to; ex.'s: CDs of bands we love, Starbucks, Google, cell phones, MTV, faces of fashion models & sporting icons; **3. i.** flight: has ↑ interaction b/t cultures, promoting shared values + attitudes; **ii.** news and entertainment industry: w/films, documentaries, quiz shows, soap operas, ads → shown around the world; **iii.** politics → dissolution of social & econ barriers: distinctive cultures & traditions have come together in a spirit of co-op; **4. i.** marketing pros need to be aware of local culture's values + buying behaviors; a product becomes a universal icon, co. has particular appeal to many ind'l cultures across globe; **ii.** marketing pros must understand diff. comm. styles ~ low-context more explicit than high-context which depends heavily on context; Ex's: instant coffee in France, Campbell Soup to Brits

Take the Unit Test

1. a 2. c 3. b 4. b 5. d 6. c 7. d 8. d 9. c 10. b

NAME _____   DATE _____

UNIT 4 TEST BUSINESS: The Art of Marketing in a Global Culture

 Listen to each question. Circle the letter of the correct answer.

1. a. flight
   b. the media
   c. political developments
   d. international business

2. a. the definition of globalization
   b. the causes of globalization
   c. ways of preventing globalization
   d. some effects of globalization

3. a. because they reflect global fads
   b. because they show common emotions
   c. because they cost millions of dollars
   d. because most cultures enjoy good soap operas

4. a. He likes them.
   b. He dislikes them.
   c. He thinks they're good for sales.
   d. He gives no indication of his feelings.

5. a. It uses famous personalities to promote ideas and products.
   b. It is supported by very large amounts of money.
   c. It uses the Internet very effectively.
   d. It spreads ideas widely and quickly.

6. a. to show that poverty is a global business concern
   b. to demonstrate how governments can improve the environment
   c. as an example of how politics contribute to globalization
   d. to explain that there are still many ideological differences in the world

7. a. as unlimited and limited
   b. as universal and limited
   c. as general and particular
   d. as universal and particular

8. a. business strategies
   b. marketing methods
   c. advertising techniques
   d. communication styles

9. a. that not everyone likes Campbell Soups
   b. that coffee is more popular
   c. that international marketing departments sometimes make mistakes
   d. that profits from international products are often lower than expected

10. a. the relationship between globalization and politics
    b. the relationship between globalization and business
    c. the importance of globalization to the entertainment industry
    d. the disadvantages of globalization

© 2009 by Pearson Education, Inc. Duplication for classroom use is permitted.

UNIT 5 COGNITIVE PSYCHOLOGY
Memory

UNIT OVERVIEW

In this unit, students work with different concepts related to human memory. The lecture itself focuses on three types of memory (sensory memory, working memory, and long-term memory) as well as two types of strategies for remembering more effectively (cognitive and affective). Follow-up projects extend the topic to issues such as the future of memory and ways to improve memory performance.

Connect to the Topic *page 42*   *~10 minutes*

Students take a survey about their memories. Survey questions concern issues such as how well students remember information and their preferred ways of remembering.

Build Your Vocabulary *pages 43–44*   *~15 minutes*

Students study the following words and phrases related to cognitive psychology and memory:

brain chemicals	implicit	relationships
come up with	implicitly agreed with	between
concerned with	logical	release
conscious	logical thought	retain
conscious effort	manipulate	seems to imply
consciously available	manipulate ideas	stored for
(to us)	manipulation of	temporarily
crucial for	psychologists	the use of logic
decade		

For the Interact with Vocabulary! activity, you may want to encourage students to first notice the boldfaced words. Knowing that the missing word is part of a collocation can help students more quickly complete the sentences.

Focus Your Attention *page 45*   *~10 minutes*

Students learn cues that lecturers use when focusing on cause-and-effect relationships:

If . . . then	*. . . causes . . .*	*. . . results in . . .*
. . . because . . .	*. . . affects . . .*	
Because of . . .	*The effect of . . .*	

Listen to the Lecture *pages 46–47*   *~30 minutes*

Students list three strategies they use for remembering information (Before You Listen) before listening to the unit lecture on memory. Students then answer fill-in-the-blank items (Listen for Main Ideas) and multiple-choice items (Listen for Details).
Lecture video time: 6 min. 24 sec.   Number of episodes: 10

Talk about the Topic *page 48*   *~20 minutes*

Four students—Rob, Alana, Ayman, and Molly—discuss the lecture. Part A focuses on matching these students with comments from the discussion. In Part B, your students work on these discussion strategies:

- Expressing an opinion: "The professor is so dry."
- Offering a fact or example: "We started meeting every Sunday at Café Roma . . ."
- Keeping the discussion on topic: "So why don't we start by going over some of the memorization strategies."

For Part C, students are encouraged to use the discussion strategies they've learned. They may use phrases from the student discussion and/or the Discussion Strategy box, or come up with their own. Encourage students to personalize their answers by referring to their own experiences learning and remembering information.
Student discussion video time: 1 min. 33 sec.

Review Your Notes *page 49*   *~15 minutes*

Students focus on reconstructing their notes, adding examples or their own comments.

BONUS ACTIVITY

As a lead-in to the unit test, you can ask the students to write three to four original factual and/or opinion questions about the lecture. They can then ask one another their questions in pairs or small groups.

Take the Unit Test *Teacher's Pack page 31*   *~15 minutes*

You may want to play the lecture again just before giving the test. Students answer standard test questions about the content of the lecture. Specifically, the test covers the following: the main points of the lecture, the three types of memory, affective strategies, verbal elaboration, the limbic system and memory, and the speaker's attitude toward memory strategies.

Extend the Topic *pages 50–51*   *~30 minutes*

- Listening and Discussion: Students listen to an interview about the future of memory, then discuss their opinions.
- Reading and Discussion: Students read and discuss a newspaper article about a man suffering from amnesia.
- Research and Presentation: Students research a technique for improving memory performance and present their findings to the class.

Focus Your Attention:
Try It Out! *page 45*

Speaker: Some people who study or work hard, drink coffee or tea because these drinks contain caffeine, and caffeine causes them to feel more energetic. And, as you would imagine, more energy allows them to study or work longer. However, did you know that caffeine may also affect memory? Researchers have found that one interesting effect of caffeine is to cause new brain cells to grow. The idea, of course, is that more brain cells might result in better memory. Actually, most researchers think that the main reason that caffeine may have a positive effect on memory is the first idea I mentioned—that caffeine gives us more energy. And more energy makes us more alert. And being more alert causes us to notice and remember more information. That seems reasonable, right? . . .

Listen for Main Ideas and Listen for Details *pages 46–47*

Cognitive psychology lecturer: E1 As part of our study of the brain's various functions, we're going to look at the topic of memory. This is a fascinating topic really. Now who remembers what they ate for lunch last Monday? I remember having pizza. That's memory at work. A simple definition of memory is the ability to store, retain, and recall the information. E2 Now, it sounds simple, but if you think about it, in many ways, we are our memories. When we think about who we are, we probably think about the events we've experienced, the people we've known, as well as the opinions and the feelings we have about a great many things. All of this information is stored in a variety of brain systems that handle the different types of memory. So first, let's look at three types of memory that have been identified by psychologists, then I'll talk about how we can improve our memories. E3 The first type of memory is sensory memory. Sensory memory is extremely short, generally lasts about 100 to 500 milliseconds. Now as the name suggests, sensory memory concerns the initial moment that we perceive something with our senses. Now, for instance, consider tactile sensory memory. If you touch a piece of silk, the memory of the smoothness of the silk will continue after you take your hand away. That's sensory memory at work. Now it's important for learning and remembering because using more senses means we've recorded the experience in more ways in our brain. E4 The next type of memory is working memory, which is extremely important in everyday life. Working memory is a system where we temporarily hold and manipulate information. You think of it as a temporary workspace in your mind. For instance, if your friend tells you a phone number and you don't have a pen, you'll probably repeat the number several times in your mind so that you remember it. In that case, you're using working memory. Now it's absolutely crucial for performing common mental operations like adding numbers, following directions, and understanding logical relationships between ideas. E5 And finally, there's what's called long-term memory, which is memory that's stored for as little as thirty seconds to as long as your entire lifetime. Now, psychologists believe that most long-term memories are information and experiences that were initially processed in working memory in meaningful and perhaps in emotional ways. For instance, I clearly remember the first time I saw the Grand Canyon. I was only fifteen years old, but the size just amazed and impressed me so much that even decades later, it's still very clear in my mind. E6 Now, there are two sub-types of long-term memory. There's declarative memory and procedural memory. Declarative memory is all of the facts, and ideas, and names that are consciously available to you. All of your experiences and conscious memories fall into this category. Procedural memory concerns your knowledge of moving your body, like when you ride a bicycle or you play a musical instrument. Most of our procedural memories are implicit and unconscious. E7 OK, now I'm going to test your memory with this question: Does anyone remember what I said I'd talk about next? How to improve your memory, right? When we think about improving our memory, we're generally talking about improving our declarative memory—the one that stores the facts, and the names, and so on. This type of memory can be improved if we use certain strategies, so I want to talk about two types of memory strategies that are useful in school: cognitive strategies and affective strategies. E8 Now, cognitive strategies tell us how to approach tasks and which methods to use to complete them. So basically, they're concerned with thinking in more effective ways. OK, let's take a quick look at one cognitive strategy. This one's called verbal elaboration. Verbal elaboration occurs when we talk in a meaningful way about information that we are trying to remember. That means that as you study, you should think about and verbalize information critically. You can use this strategy by agreeing or disagreeing with the information, or by comparing and contrasting the information to ideas you already know, or by discussing relationships between ideas. When we make meaningful relationships between what we already know and what we are trying to learn, we'll remember more and we'll remember it longer.

E9 Now, for the other approach: affective strategies. Affective strategies help us control our emotional responses so that we remember better. But what do emotions have to do with memories? Well, emotions cause the release of brain chemicals that play a direct role in memory formation. And part of the emotion system in the brain, called "the limbic system," helps transfer information into long-term memory. In other words, how you feel about something affects how well you remember it.

E10 So, what affective strategies can you use to create positive emotional responses while studying? First, study with one or two friends from class. This can make any study session more interesting and more enjoyable. Second, use interesting study tasks, like taking turns making short presentations on the topic that you're studying. Or come up with questions to test each other on the information. See, the point of trying the affective strategy is that it will increase not only your memory, but also your sense of fun, and challenge, and interest. And you can do this for any subject. Now, are there any questions?

Coaching Tips

[1] Critical Thinking: Predicting At the start of his lecture, the speaker says that his topic will be memory. He goes on to say that people store information "in a variety of brain systems that handle different types of memory." Using this new information, can you can make any predictions about what the lecture will cover? Probably a discussion of brain systems and types of memory, right? Try getting into the habit of predicting what you're about to hear. You'll be better prepared for the new information, and you may be surprised at how good at it you are!

Find audioscript for the other Coaching Tips at www.pearsonlongman.com/contemporarytopics.

Talk about the Topic *page 48*

Rob: So why don't we start by going over some of the memorization strategies.

Alana: Uh-huh.

Rob: So, guys, does anyone think that any of these memorization strategies actually work? Like, do any of you actually practice any of them?

Alana: Yeah, I do.

Rob: You do?

Alana: I use the cognitive one. What did he call it? Verbal something?

Molly: Oh, I have that here. Verbal elaboration.

Alana: That's it. I have used it in my art history class. After class, I have a little conversation with myself, think about what I like and don't like and why. It's really helped me feel more familiar with the material.

Molly: Well, isn't that kind of common sense? I mean, duh, think about what you've read and heard; don't just memorize it.

Ayman: Well, it's kind of different for me. I grew up learning everything via memorization. Just memorizing it. Which is a good approach with some things.

Rob: What about the affective strategy that he mentioned? Like, do any of you think that you can actually change your feelings about a subject?

Ayman: That's a tough one. Like, I'm taking this philosophy class now. I just can't get into it—the professor is so dry.

Molly: This might help: Last semester, this guy I sat next to in statistics. We started meeting every Sunday at Café Roma to study, and we'd have questions prepared for each other and stuff, and it totally helped me survive that class.

Ayman: Oh. So you're saying it's smart to first think about who you're going to sit by in class.

Molly: No!

Rob: Exactly!

Molly: OK, that is inferring something.

Rob: Now we see the truth!

Take the Unit Test

1. What are the two main points of the lecture?
2. Which of the following topics does the speaker *not* discuss?
3. Where are memories stored?
4. What is the correct order of memory systems, from shortest to longest?
5. Improving memory primarily concerns which type of memory?
6. Which of the following was *not* mentioned as an example of verbal elaboration?
7. How is the limbic system related to memory formation?
8. Which of the following is probably true about memory?
9. A study group creates quiz questions for each other. Which are they using?
10. What is the speaker's attitude toward using memory strategies?

Extend the Topic *page 50*

Marshall: Thanks for being here today, Aisha. So tell our listeners, what exactly is meant by "the future of memory"?

Aisha: Well, first it means that our understanding of memory is changing. Memory is now seen as extending beyond our mind. Obviously, our memories exist in our minds, but they also exist in our environment.

Marshall: Like, when I write something down on a piece of paper?

Aisha: Yes, that's a good example. But an even better example might be computers, or technology in general. And that brings us to the second point about "the future of memory." Technology is changing our conception of memory.

Marshall: Hmm. Could you give an example of that?

Aisha: Sure. Just look at computers. Huge amounts of information can be kept on these devices, right? For instance, we can have the names and e-mail addresses of thousands of people with us at all times.

Marshall: So, you're saying the information on the computer would be considered part of our memory?

Aisha: Yes, exactly. It's an extension of our biological memory. And future technology will have an even stronger impact on us. For example, in the future, we'll wear eyeglasses that have automatic face recognition. If you see someone you met several years ago, the eyeglasses will show you the results of a database search. If the face is identified, then the person's name will be shown on the inside of the glasses.

Marshall: That's amazing! So the future of memory is an increasingly seamless integration between memories in our brain and information available on high-tech devices.

Aisha: Right. And "seamless" is the key word there . . .

ANSWER KEY

Build Your Vocabulary *pages 43–44*

B. 1. f 2. d 3. b 4. e 5. i 6. a 7. j 8. g 9. h 10. c
C. 1. N 2. A 3. N 4. A 5. A 6. V 7. N 8. V 9. V
10. AV **D. Interactive Vocabulary!** 1. consciously
2. conscious 3. implicitly 4. imply 5. logical
6. logic 7. manipulate 8. manipulation

Focus Your Attention *page 45*

A. Phrases: because; causes; affect; effect; cause;
result in; reason that; effect; causes; Causes-Effects:
caffeine-energetic; more energy-work longer;
caffeine-better memory/more alert

Listen for Main Ideas *page 46*

B. 1. store, retain, recall 2. initial moment, senses
3. hold, manipulate 4. meaningful, emotional
5. consciously available 6. implicit, unconscious
7. Cognitive strategies 8. Affective strategies

Listen for Details *page 47*

B. 1. c 2. c 3. b 4. c 5. b 6. b 7. a 8. a

Talk about the Topic *page 48*

A. 1. Alana 2. Molly 3. Alana, Ayman 4. Ayman,
Molly **B.** Expressing an opinion: 3; Offering a fact
or example: 4; Keeping the discussion on topic: 1, 2

Review Your Notes *page 49*

3 memory systems: (1) sensory, (2) working,
(3) long-term; **Diff's:** declarative memories =
conscious; procedural memories = implicit &
unconscious; **cognitive strategies** help us think in
more effective ways; ex: verbal elaboration;
affective strategies help us control our emotional
responses so that we remember better; ex: studying
w/friends & using interesting study tasks

Take the Unit Test

1. b 2. b 3. d 4. a 5. d 6. c 7. d 8. d 9. c 10. d

UNIT 5 TEST COGNITIVE PSYCHOLOGY: Memory

Listen to each question. Circle the letter of the correct answer.

1. a. sensory memory and working memory
   b. types of memory and memory strategies
   c. declarative and procedural memory
   d. cognitive and affective strategies

2. a. sensory memory
   b. auditory memory
   c. brain chemicals
   d. the limbic system

3. a. in the working memory system
   b. in the declarative memory system
   c. in the procedural memory system
   d. in a variety of memory systems

4. a. sensory memory, working memory, long-term memory
   b. sensory memory, long-term memory, working memory
   c. working memory, sensory memory, long-term memory
   d. long-term memory, working memory, sensory memory

5. a. sensory memory
   b. working memory
   c. procedural memory
   d. declarative memory

6. a. agreeing and disagreeing with information
   b. comparing and contrasting information
   c. reviewing information repeatedly
   d. discussing relationships between ideas

7. a. It is a part of sensory memory.
   b. It is used for verbal elaboration.
   c. It plays a key role in procedural memory.
   d. It helps transfer information into long-term memory.

8. a. Not everyone uses sensory memory.
   b. Most people do not use working memory very often.
   c. People who use good strategies can remember nearly everything.
   d. People remember more when they process information more deeply.

9. a. sensory memory
   b. a cognitive strategy
   c. an affective strategy
   d. an ineffective way to remember information

10. a. He is skeptical of their value.
    b. He believes that most people misuse them.
    c. He appears neutral.
    d. He believes that they are useful.

UNIT 6 ANTHROPOLOGY/BIOLOGY
The Science of Love

TEACHING TIPS

UNIT OVERVIEW

In this unit, students learn how falling in love has the same characteristics as many rituals, and how there is a biochemical basis of romantic love. The lecture focuses on four major characteristics of rituals as they apply to falling in love, and three major biochemical phases that people pass through, each of which involves different brain chemicals and/or hormones. Follow-up projects extend the topic to alternative explanations for the phenomenon of romantic love and romantic love as portrayed in films and books.

Connect to the Topic   *page 52*   *~10 minutes*

Students take a survey about their beliefs concerning love. Survey questions concern issues such as the universality of romantic love and the degree to which love can be explained in rational or scientific terms.

Build Your Vocabulary   *pages 53–54*   *~15 minutes*

Students study the following words and phrases related to anthropology, biology, and love:

anthropologists	enhance	(the) notion of
attached to	enhance feelings of	phase of
attachment	express emotions	prospective
basis for	flooded by	resistance to
characteristic	hormone	romantic
dominant in	invoke	symbols of (love)
emotion	mutual	a tolerance to

For the Interact with Vocabulary! activity, you may want to encourage students to first notice the boldfaced words. Figuring out these collocations can help students more quickly unscramble the sentences.

Focus Your Attention   *page 55*   *~10 minutes*

Students learn cues that lecturers use when giving information in the form of a list:

. . . three causes for . . .   *. . . three major characteristics of . . .*
. . . four important effects of . . .   *. . . four types of . . .*

Listen to the Lecture   *pages 56–57*   *~30 minutes*

Students preview terms from the lecture (Before You Listen) before listening to the unit lecture on love. Students then answer true/false items (Listen for Main Ideas) and fill-in-the-blank items (Listen for Details).
Lecture video time: 5 min. 48 sec.   Number of episodes: 9

Talk about the Topic   *page 58*   *~20 minutes*

Four students—River, Hannah, Mia, and Manny—discuss the lecture. Part A focuses on matching these students with ideas from the discussion. In Part B, your students work on these discussion strategies:

- Asking for opinions or ideas: "Who agrees with the idea that love is the result of a biochemical process?"
- Disagreeing: "I don't think she was saying that."
- Trying to reach a consensus: "Can we at least agree that we do have some control?"

For Part C, students are encouraged to use the discussion strategies they've learned. They may use phrases from the student discussion and/or the Discussion Strategy box, or come up with their own. Keep in mind that some students may be reluctant to talk about love and romantic relationships while others are eager to talk about them.
Student discussion video time: 1 min. 33 sec.

Review Your Notes   *page 59*   *~15 minutes*

Students focus on reconstructing their notes, paying attention to the two lists (the four stages of a ritual and the three biochemical phases of love) provided in the lecture.

BONUS ACTIVITY

As a lead-in to the unit test, you can ask the students to consider how daily activities do or do not display the four characteristics of a ritual. For instance, how does attending a class involve (a) face-to-face contact, (b) a common object or activity, (c) a mutual emotion, and (d) an emotionally charged symbol? How is the daily activity similar to or different from the ritual described in the lecture?

Take the Unit Test   *Teacher's Pack page 37*   *~15 minutes*

You may want to play the lecture again just before giving the test. Students answer standard test questions about the content of the lecture. Specifically, the test covers the following: the main points of the lecture, the order of topics in the lecture, characteristics of a ritual, the three biochemical phases of love, the effects of specific brain chemicals, and the reason for decreasing levels of euphoria.

Extend the Topic   *pages 60–61*   *~30 minutes*

- Listening and Discussion: Students listen to and discuss a reading by the author of a book on men's and women's attitudes toward romance.
- Reading and Discussion: Students read about and discuss explanations from different academic fields for why people fall in love.
- Research and Presentation: Students research a film or novel involving a romantic relationship and discuss it with the class in terms of their own culture.

Focus Your Attention:
Try It Out! *page 55*

Speaker: All right. Now, one well-known psychologist, Robert Sternberg, has proposed a theory of love in the context of interpersonal relationships. He proposes that there are three kinds of interpersonal love. The first is intimacy, which concerns feelings of closeness and connectedness. Most of us feel this type of love with friends and family. The second is passion. As you might expect, this involves feelings of romance and physical attraction toward another person. The third and final type of love is commitment. This means that there's a commitment to maintain the relationship over a long period. Sternberg believes that relationships based on at least two of these types will last much longer than relationships based only on one of them . . .

Listen for Main Ideas and Listen for Details *pages 56–57*

Anthropology/Biology lecturer: E1 Who here has seen a romantic comedy or read a romance novel, or even met a special someone, and felt that "tug" of romantic love? Most of you, but maybe not all. Just how universal is this notion of romantic love? Any ideas? Well, anthropologists have identified romantic love in almost every human culture. For instance, one recent study showed that 147 out of 166 cultures had some form of romantic love. This suggests that romantic love is at least partly biologically based. There's also a social "science" to romantic love, which is where I'm going to begin today. E2 Anthropologists describe romantic love as a high-intensity social ritual, a ritual being a prescribed form of conducting a formal ceremony. Now this may seem surprising because we aren't usually aware of following any kinds of "rules" when we fall in love. But in fact, falling in love does have the four major characteristics of a ritual. The first characteristic of a ritual is that it brings people into face-to-face contact. Clearly, romantic love does this. People who are in love want to spend as much time together as possible. The second characteristic of a ritual is that it focuses people's attention on some common object or activity. With romantic love, the common object is the couple itself. For people in love, other people and activities seem to fade away. E3 Now, the third characteristic of a ritual is that it promotes a mutual emotion among the participants. Obviously, romantic love qualifies here. Few other experiences can surpass it in

intensity. This is why romantic love is described as a "high-intensity" ritual. The final characteristic of a ritual is that it produces an emotionally charged symbol that represents membership in some group. Well, what are some of the symbols in romantic love? In Western cultures, love is associated with heart-shaped objects and rings. For instance, a wedding ring symbolizes the couple's love and commitment. And we all know how important these symbols can be. For instance, losing a ring, for example, can cause a lot of anxiety, so be careful with those symbols! E4 Now let's look at what's happening in your brain and in your body when you feel the emotion that we call romantic love. Recent research indicates that there's a biochemical basis to love, so there's a good reason why people in love feel as if they're in a different and more beautiful world—their brain is literally flooded by hormones and chemicals that cause them to feel the way they feel. We can break the process of falling in love into three fairly distinct phases based on the hormones and chemicals dominant in each phase. E5 In the first phase, the hormones testosterone and estrogen play important roles. Although testosterone has a reputation as a male hormone, it is also present in women. And it has many effects on the brain, one of which is to make us seek partners and to be alert to the presence of possible partners. So in essence, these hormones get us out looking for and then noticing prospective partners to fall in love with. E6 It's in the second phase where people have the feeling of being in love. Here, some powerful amphetamines are released into the brain. Amphetamines are a kind of stimulant, right? They make us feel alert. Well, two of these amphetamines are dopamine and phenylethylamine, also known as PEA. Dopamine has a physical effect on our body—it increases our heart rate and blood pressure, and seems to make us more talkative. It also has a powerful psychological effect, invoking feelings of pleasure and excitement, and it enhances our emotional responses to things. E7 The other chemical released in this phase is PEA. PEA is a neurotransmitter, which means it increases the electrical signals between the neurons in the brain. This makes us feel euphoric—it's the chemical that makes us smile a lot when we're first in love, and feel like we're in some kind of heavenly world. But because our body develops a tolerance to PEA, the euphoric feelings gradually disappear. E8 And that brings us to the final phase of love, which is concerned with longer lasting commitment and attachment. The first important compound in this stage is endorphins. Endorphins are natural painkillers that give us a sense of security, and feelings of peace and calm—they basically improve our mood. Our brain also secretes hormones that play a role in the formation of social attachments.

One such hormone is oxytocin—sometimes called "the cuddle chemical." Oxytocin seems to produce the feelings of relaxed satisfaction and attachment to another person. E9 Now, as you might imagine, there is some resistance to the idea of love being determined by brain chemistry and hormones. Do you know where this resistance might come from?

Coaching Tips
[1] Listening: Recognizing rhetorical questions
The speaker asks, "Just how universal is this notion of romantic love? Any ideas?" Do you think she wants you to answer aloud? When speakers ask rhetorical questions, they don't expect you to answer. Rather, they use these questions to pique your interest in the topic and/or to introduce their next point. Thinking about the answers to such questions can help you focus on the topic and get ready to hear what comes next.
Find audioscript for the other Coaching Tips at www.pearsonlongman.com/contemporarytopics.

Talk about the Topic *page 58*
Hannah: Who agrees with the idea that love is the result of a biochemical process?

Mia: I do. Absolutely! If you've ever been in love, you know that kind of "drugged" sensation she mentioned. That's the chemicals and hormones at work!

River: Well, I've had some romantic experiences. I wouldn't say I've ever been "drugged" by anyone.

Mia: Really? Well, what about that first phase she mentioned—the one where you're looking for a partner, you know, seeking a partner? Surely you've experienced that part.

River: Actually, I don't do much seeking. I'm usually the one being sought.

Manny: Well, that makes sense. After all, it takes all kinds to make the love ritual work.

Hannah: And what about you? Have you experienced the three phases of falling in love?

Manny: Well, not so much for myself, but I know about the third stage—the commitment stage—from watching my older brother and his wife. They've been married for like five years, and they're content. I'd say happy. They're not real passionate, but I'd say happy. That's, uh, oxytocin. That's oxytocin working.

Hannah: Well, personally, I resist the idea that love is completely chemical or hormonal. I mean, we're not animals, right?

Mia: I don't think she was saying that.

Hannah: Well, maybe not. But can we at least agree that we do have some control? I mean, we may have these feelings, but we can consciously control them, right?

Mia: Yeah, of course!

River: Well, of course. Definitely. I mean . . .

Take the Unit Test
1. What are the two main points of the lecture?
2. What is one purpose of a wedding ring?
3. Why is romantic love described as a "high-intensity ritual"?
4. In what order does the speaker talk about the biochemical basis of love?
5. Which of the following is associated with the first biochemical phase of love?
6. Which is *not* a physical effect of dopamine?
7. Why do euphoric feelings of love gradually disappear?
8. What is the main effect of endorphins?
9. Which of the following about love is probably true?
10. What would the speaker probably think about the idea that love will never be understood by scientists?

Extend the Topic *page 60*
Author: Thank you. Well, let me give you some background before I read. I was inspired to write this book after attending a conference in Miami. There I heard experts in psychology, sociology, and biology present on romance and how the two genders perceive it differently. Their conclusions? Well, some of the differences are caused by nature and others by nurture. But the big question was how much of each? On that question, few of the experts could agree. Hence, my inspiration to research it further, and write a book! So on that note, I'd like to read you a short excerpt, starting on page 14. "On one hand, some scientists make the point that the brains of boys and girls are awash in very different hormones throughout their entire lives. They also note that the left and right hemispheres of women's brains are more highly connected, a fact that usually is interpreted to mean that women's thinking is more strongly connected to their emotions. So we know that there are some real physical differences behind how men and women experience romance. On the other hand, socialization undoubtedly also plays a role in each gender's approach to romance. Some experts say that the fact that women are generally more comfortable expressing affection toward men than men are toward women is the result of socialization. Another behavior attributed to socialization is women's comfort with expressing fear and sadness, regardless of the gender of the person they're talking to. This isn't the case with men. So how much of the difference is attributed to nature and how much to nurture? Opinions and evidence vary. One famous study, conducted in . . .

ANSWER KEY

Build Your Vocabulary *pages 53–54*

A. 1. people, societies, beliefs 2. loyalty, love, friendship 3. quality, feature 4. strong human feeling 5. make it better 6. growth, development, health 7. causes, to happen 8. felt, done, one another 9. likely, do, likely to happen 10. love, words, actions **D. Interact with Vocabulary!** 1. the notion of romantic love 2. there is a biological basis for 3. is that they are attached to 4. often express their emotions to the person 5. be careful with any symbols of love 6. is flooded by many chemicals 7. are dominant in each phase of 8. enhance mutual feelings of attraction 9. a tolerance to some hormones 10. some resistance to the idea that

Focus Your Attention *page 55*

A. 1. intimacy: feelings of closeness and connectedness (e.g., with friends or family); 2. passion: feelings of romance and physical attraction toward another person; 3. commitment: a commitment to maintain the relationship over a long period

Listen for Main Ideas *page 56*

B. 1. F (not half—147 of 166) 2. F (standard, not optional) 3. T 4. T 5. T 6. T 7. T (Note: students may argue for "false" because of the incompleteness of the statement. Amphetamines also cause increased heart rate and blood pressure, and feelings of euphoria.) 8. F (endorphins and hormones like oxytocin are released)

Listen for Details *page 57*

B. 1. biologically based 2. ritual 3. heart-shaped object 4. Testosterone 5. Amphetamines 6. Dopamine 7. PEA 8. Endorphins 9. Oxytocin

Talk about the Topic *page 58*

A. 1. Mia 2. Hannah 3. River, Hannah, Mia
B. Asking for opinions or ideas: 1; Disagreeing: 2, 3; Trying to reach a consensus: 4

Review Your Notes *page 59*

4 characteristics of a ritual (1) brings people into face-to-face contact, (2) focuses people's attn. on a common object/ activity, (3) promotes a mutual emotion among the participants, (4) produces an emotionally charged symbol; **3 biochemical phases:** (1) testosterone and estrogen are released & people look for prospective partners, (2) amphetamines ~ dopamine + PEA are released + make people feel good, (3) endorphins make people feel calm; the hormone oxytocin makes them feel satisfied/ attached to the other person

Take the Unit Test

1. b 2. b 3. c 4. a 5. d 6. c 7. d 8. b 9. d 10. a

UNIT 6 TEST ANTHROPOLOGY/BIOLOGY: The Science of Love

Listen to each question. Circle the letter of the correct answer.

1. a. love as a social ritual and long-term relationships
   b. love as a social ritual and the biochemical basis of love
   c. the universality of love and long-term relationships
   d. the universality of love and the symbolic nature of love

2. a. to inform others of a couple's love
   b. to symbolize a couple's love
   c. to increase the intensity of a couple's love
   d. to influence the production of hormones

3. a. because most people fall in love infrequently
   b. because love often leads to long-term relationships
   c. because love is an extremely powerful emotion
   d. because intense feelings of love occur for a short amount of time

4. a. alertness, feelings of pleasure, commitment
   b. feelings of pleasure, alertness, commitment
   c. feelings of pleasure, commitment, alertness
   d. commitment, alertness, feelings of pleasure

5. a. amphetamines
   b. neurotransmitters
   c. oxytocin
   d. testosterone

6. a. higher heart rate
   b. higher blood pressure
   c. increased nervousness
   d. increased talkativeness

7. a. because fewer hormones are secreted
   b. because fewer amphetamines are secreted
   c. because our body develops a tolerance to dopamine
   d. because our body develops a tolerance to PEA

8. a. feelings of alertness
   b. feelings of peace and calm
   c. feelings of love
   d. feelings of detachment

9. a. Everyone will fall in love at least once.
   b. Women fall in love more easily than men.
   c. Romantic love is an unnatural phenomenon.
   d. Feelings of love are not completely under our control.

10. a. She would disagree.
    b. She would have no opinion.
    c. She would agree.
    d. She would say that no one knows.

TEACHING TIPS

UNIT OVERVIEW

The main focus of this unit is the possibility of humankind making a trip to the planet Mars (and back) with the purpose of setting up a colony. It considers, in particular, the challenges such a trip would entail. A section of the lecture and Extend the Topic encourage students to focus on reasons why such a trip might become a necessity in the future, considering in particular the environmental dangers that threaten to make Earth uninhabitable.

Connect to the Topic *page 62*   *~10 minutes*

Students are invited to consider and list some of the advantages and disadvantages of space exploration. Students discuss their results as a class.

Build Your Vocabulary *pages 63–64*   *~15 minutes*

Students study the following words and phrases related to astronomy and space exploration:

alternative to		
bureaucratic	essential	overcome
challenge of	facilities	resources
concerned about	gone away	sustainable
contender for	maintain	unreliable
detecting	obstacles to	vehicle

Focus Your Attention *page 65*   *~10 minutes*

Students look at the importance of organizing notes on their page so that they become a visual map of the lecture, moving from left to right as ideas become more detailed. You may wish to briefly introduce students to alternative methods of organization, such as spidergrams. Students then listen to information presented in an audio clip and make notes, organizing them in the way described.

Listen to the Lecture *pages 66–67*   *~30 minutes*

Students list four challenges of a trip to Mars (Before You Listen) before listening to the unit lecture on space travel to Mars. Students then answer true/false items (Listen for Main Ideas) and multiple-choice items (Listen for Details).
Lecture video time: 7 min. 2 sec.   *Number of episodes: 10*

Talk about the Topic   *page 68*   *~20 minutes*

Four students—Alana, Ayman, Molly, and Rob—discuss interplanetary travel. Part A focuses on matching these students with ideas from the discussion. In Part B, your students work on these discussion strategies:

- Expressing an opinion: "You guys are a bunch of fatalists."
- Disagreeing: "No, no. Come on."
- Keeping the discussion on topic: "So, does anyone want to review the lecture?"

For Part C, students are encouraged to use the discussion strategies they've learned. They may use phrases from the student discussion and/or the Discussion Strategy box, or come up with their own.
Student discussion video time: 1 min. 13 sec.

Review Your Notes   *page 69*   *~15 minutes*

Students focus on reconstructing their notes, paying particular attention to layout, as discussed in Focus Your Attention.

BONUS ACTIVITY

Have students work in pairs and present a coherent summary of the lecture to one another using their completed notes.

Take the Unit Test   *Teacher's Pack page 43*   *~15 minutes*

You want to play the lecture again just before giving the test. Students answer standard test questions about the content of the lecture. Specifically, the test covers the following: reasons for colonizing other planets, obstacles to a mission to Mars, types of spacecraft and propulsion methods, supplies and their use, the lecturer's feelings and language, and the main idea of the lecture.

Extend the Topic   *pages 70–71*   *~30 minutes*

- Listening and Discussion: Students listen to and discuss a blogcast on the importance of space exploration.
- Reading and Discussion: Students read about and discuss four initiatives designed to reduce environmental damage to Earth.
- Research and Presentation: Students research a space mission and present their findings to the class.

Focus Your Attention:
Try It Out! *page 65*

Speaker: So, there are a couple of things to consider. To start with, there's the cost. Space exploration is notoriously expensive, and that raises at least two important—and related—questions. First, should we really give priority to expensive space projects when we have more immediate problems to solve here on our own planet? I'm talking about a lack of schools and good healthcare, and starving populations, to name a few. Secondly, why aren't the billions of dollars invested in space projects used to solve Earth's environmental challenges? In other words, if we invest in solving Earth's problems, then we eliminate one of the main arguments for space exploration—colonization. Besides, that "solution" may be decades, if not centuries, away anyway. OK, so that's cost. Next, is the inherent danger of space travel. Every time we send astronauts into space . . .

Listen for Main Ideas and Listen
for Details *pages 66–67*

Astronomy lecturer: E1 We all know that space travel is dangerous. But despite the dangers highlighted by the two space shuttle tragedies and all the problems that have beleaguered the International Space Station, our curiosity and desire to explore the universe is alive and well. Just witness China, Japan, and Europe's new space programs. The initial spirit of the Apollo missions of the '60s and '70s hasn't gone away. Far from it. E2 And, as I'm sure many of you have thought about, that spirit of exploration isn't just the result of romantic notions of space travel and discovering life on other planets. I hate to say it, but it reflects a growing realization that at some point in the future—and it may be closer than we think—we'll have to colonize other planets. Why? Out of necessity. Because, as Earth's resources run out—and if our climate continues to change—life here simply won't be sustainable. E3 So, with that in mind, I'd like us to consider the planet Mars as a contender for a possible space colony, and I'd like to outline some of the obstacles that would need to be overcome if we're going to send astronauts to Mars to get things started. So far only robots have been sent. I'm going to look at three obstacles. One: designing and building a spacecraft that could get astronauts to Mars in one piece. Two: an effective method of propulsion. And three: the supply of water, fuel, air, and food needed. E4 First, let's look at the design of the spacecraft. Well, right away, scientists know that a winged aircraft like the space shuttle isn't an option. Why? Because the Martian atmosphere is just too thin—the wings wouldn't support the shuttle because they wouldn't get enough lift from the air. Result? The craft would simply plummet to the ground. Plus, even on short trips the shuttle is beginning to look pretty unreliable. So, what's the alternative? OK, well it looks as though some kind of capsule, like the ones used in the Gemini and Apollo programs, is a real possibility. These capsules proved to be strong and safe, particularly during the critical—and very dangerous—first and last 100 miles of space missions. In fact, work is already being done to develop a capsule-like crew transfer vehicle to carry astronauts to and from the International Space Station. Are you with me? E5 Well, then let's move on to the second challenge, namely propulsion. You've got your spacecraft. Now, how do you power it all the way to Mars and back? Whatever power source you use, it needs to be reliable, safe, and fast. After all, the astronauts don't want to spend any longer than necessary in such a small vehicle. Would you? Plus, the longer they're in deep space, the longer they're exposed to dangerous radiation. So, what are the options? Well, there are three options, but none are perfect. The first option is an ion-propulsion engine. Now, for this kind of engine, a portable nuclear reactor heats charged gas and then fires it out of the rear of the spacecraft. That's ion propulsion. Do you know what I mean? The main advantage of this kind of engine is that it can accelerate the craft to very high speeds. The disadvantage is that it's slow to accelerate. And as we've seen, time is important and needs to be minimized on such a long journey. E6 The second option is nuclear thermal propulsion. This kind of engine uses a nuclear reactor to heat propellant and blast it out of the engine nozzle. Are you following? Advantage: This system gets the craft moving much faster. Disadvantage: It's heavier and worries environmentalists who are concerned about a possible nuclear disaster before the rocket even leaves the atmosphere. E7 The third possible option is a plasma propulsion rocket. Now, this kind of engine is currently being developed by NASA and can get astronauts to Mars in just forty days. Very impressive! This system uses magnets and gas to produce acceleration. There are no obvious disadvantages except that it will take several more years to develop. E8 A bigger problem than either the spacecraft or propulsion method, though, is the water, fuel, air, and food a mission to Mars would require. Unlike the Apollo trips, which lasted a maximum of twelve days, a round-trip to Mars would take about fourteen months. You then have to add to that another eighteen months on the planet itself waiting for the next moment when the positions of the Earth and Mars would allow for a return home. So, you see, in total a trip to Mars would take nearly three years. This presents a big problem for scientists who need to minimize the weight while also ensuring that the astronauts have the water, fuel, air, and food they need. And they can't simply build a larger ship to carry all the cargo as this would require a rocket so large it would probably be impossible to launch. **E9** So, what are the alternatives? One possibility would be to manufacture a lot of what's needed on Mars itself rather than here on Earth. Detecting water on the planet in advance would be essential for this option. For starters, the water, once purified, could be used for drinking and bathing. And, what's more, the hydrogen and oxygen that make up the water could be used to propel the liquid fuel engines of the ship for the return to Earth. Of course, astronauts would need to have a facility to manufacture the fuel. But assuming that that could be done, then they could fill up the fuel tanks and return home. Do you see where I'm going with this? The oxygen could also be used to create and maintain a breathable atmosphere on Mars. And the thing is, once you've come up with a solution for the water, fuel, and air problems, you've pretty much also come up with a solution to the food problem. After all, if you're able to produce these things on Mars, then throw sunlight into the mix and you've got practically all you need to grow food. So you can see that although there are plenty of ifs and buts, here's a neat solution to a number of the key problems, right? **E10** To sum up then, the goal of colonizing the Red Planet is almost within reach it seems, but, like I said, there are lots of ifs and buts. And it'll take time. I'd say that perhaps the greatest obstacle of all is something I haven't mentioned, and that's the political and bureaucratic one. While the technical obstacles might be overcome, I suspect that the political and bureaucratic one won't be so easy!

Coaching Tips

[1] Note-taking: Organizing ideas There are many ways to organize your notes. For instance, you might use bullets, arrows, and other symbols. Or you might prefer the more formal outline style, with numbers and letters. Choose a style that suits you. What's most important is that you capture the main ideas and details, and that you show how ideas relate. Also important is organizing your notes neatly and logically so that you can review them with ease. Here's a basic structure you can follow for organizing your notes: [see video for note-taking example].

Find audioscript for the other Coaching Tips at www.pearsonlongman.com/contemporarytopics.

Talk about the Topic   *page 68*

Alana: As I see it, this whole idea of traveling to other planets and setting up colonies is based on one big assumption.

Ayman: What's that? That we'll actually come up with the technology to do it?

Alana: No. She's making the assumption that Earth is no longer going to be inhabitable some day. That we'll have to start living on other planets. So why do we assume that?

Molly: Well, you know: climate change, pollution, over-population, war!

Rob: Exactly. And people keep living longer and longer. So, eventually, we're going to have to go somewhere else. We won't have a choice.

Alana: You guys are a bunch of fatalists.

Molly: Or realists!

Alana: No, no. Come on. She also said that, oh yeah, that humans have a desire to explore. You know, the "human spirit of exploration"!

Rob: Sure, I guess so.

Ayman: So, does anyone want to review the lecture? The design of the spacecraft, the types of propulsion, any of that?

Molly: It's kind of a hard lecture.

Ayman: No, it's not that hard. It's just basic problem solving. It's not rocket science!

Rob: Yes, it is rocket science, as a matter of fact.

Ayman: Oh yeah, yeah. You're right. It is!

Take the Unit Test

1. Why do we need to colonize other planets?
2. What three main obstacles of a mission to Mars did the speaker cover?
3. Why is a capsule preferable to the space shuttle for a trip to Mars?
4. What is the main advantage of a plasma propulsion rocket?
5. Why would a Mars mission probably take longer than the Apollo missions did?
6. The speaker mentions two uses for the oxygen and hydrogen that would come from water detected on Mars. What are they? Choose *two* answers.
7. What problem does having water, air, and sunlight solve?
8. What does the speaker feel might be the most difficult problem to overcome for a Mars mission?
9. The speaker says there are lots of "ifs and buts" involved in getting to Mars. What does she mean?
10. What is the main idea of the lecture?

Extend the Topic *page 70*

Blogcaster: Michael, what would you say to those people—often politicians—who argue that space exploration is an unnecessary extravagance. That the huge sums of money invested in space projects could be better spent on schools, hospitals, and poverty issues?

Michael: Well, I'd say this: It's a fact that exploration is an important survival strategy in evolution. Species migrate to find new food sources and safe habitats. They also migrate when population pressures and environmental factors force them to. Just look at endangered species like polar bears. Increasingly, they're showing up in human settlements which are not natural to them. But they've got no choice! As their environment is shrinking, so too are their natural food sources.

Blogcaster: So are you suggesting that the same pressures or factors will eventually force the human species to look for new habitats—new worlds—in order to survive?

Michael: That's exactly what I'm saying. But that's not the only argument for space exploration. There's also what I call the "curiosity factor." You see, humans have an intellectual urge to explore the unknown. In the past, that's meant Mount Everest, the polar caps, the Americas, and so on. In the twenty-first century, the ultimate frontier for exploration is space. Satellites and so on can only tell us so much. And so if we really want to find out about other worlds, we've got to go there. It's as simple as that.

ANSWER KEY

Build Your Vocabulary *pages 63–64*

B. 1. c 2. c 3. b 4. c 5. b 6. b 7. b 8. a 9. a
10. a **C. Interact with Vocabulary!** 1. to 2. about
3. for 4. away 5. to 6. of

Focus Your Attention *page 65*

A. I. Space exploration $$$
   1) Solve immediate problems
      ex. schools, healthcare, starving
      populations
   2) Solve Earth's env't problems = elim.
      colonization argument
  II. Space travel = dangerous

Listen for Main Ideas *page 66*

B. 1. F (to determine if it's inhabitable) 2. F (and propulsion, not astronauts' health) 3. T 4. T 5. T
6. F (technical challenges easier than political and bureaucratic)

Listen for Details *page 67*

B. 1. c 2. c 3. b 4. a 5. b 6. b 7. a 8. c

Talk about the Topic *page 68*

A. 1. Alana 2. Molly, Rob 3. Molly 4. Ayman
B. Expressing an opinion: 1, 2, 4; Disagreeing: 1, 2, 4; Keeping the discussion on topic: 3

Review Your Notes *page 69*

Space travel is not just a luxury, it's a necessity:
              Earth's resources running out
                 climate changing
Mars = best candidate for a space colony:
              potential for water
              close by
          robots have been there
3 main obstacles to a Martian mission:
          1. designing + building spacecraft
          2. effect method of propulsion
          3. supply of water, fuel, air, food
Political and bureaucratic challenges:
   Not covered in lecture. Students can brainstorm their own ideas.

Take the Unit Test

1. c 2. c 3. b 4. c 5. a 6. b and d 7. c 8. d 9. d
10. a

 **TEST** ASTRONOMY: Mission to Mars

 Listen to each question. Circle the letter of the correct answer.

1. a. because humankind has a natural desire to explore

   b. because people still have romantic notions of space travel

   c. because eventually life on Earth won't be sustainable

   d. because technology now allows us to do so as never before

2. a. spacecraft, highly skilled astronauts, supplies

   b. spacecraft, propulsion method, political support

   c. spacecraft, propulsion, supplies

   d. propulsion, supplies, highly skilled astronauts

3. a. because it's cheaper to produce

   b. because it's better suited to the Martian atmosphere

   c. because it's more spacious

   d. because it's faster and easier to control

4. a. It's cheap to produce.

   b. It's reliable.

   c. It's very fast.

   d. It's environmentally safe.

5. a. because the distance to Mars is greater

   b. because rockets are faster now

   c. because fuel wasn't a problem before

   d. because the Apollo astronauts wanted to return early

6. a. food storage

   b. a breathable atmosphere

   c. medicines

   d. powering the engines

7. a. breathing

   b. sleep

   c. food

   d. fuel

8. a. the cost

   b. getting public support

   c. food

   d. getting political support

9. a. There are many organizations involved.

   b. There are many people who oppose the idea.

   c. There are many people who believe a mission to Mars is impossible.

   d. There are many conditions that need to be met.

10. a. There are numerous challenges and solutions to colonizing Mars.

   b. Humankind will never have the technology necessary to colonize Mars.

   c. Only politics is preventing humankind from colonizing Mars.

   d. Space shuttle missions prove that it is possible to set up a colony on Mars.

POLITICAL SCIENCE: Big Brother and the Surveillance Society

UNIT OVERVIEW

In this unit, students will look at the increasingly widespread use of surveillance mechanisms that enable political, commercial, and security organizations to track our movements and behavior. The lecture focuses on some of the most common mechanisms and the issue of invasion of privacy—also covered in Extend the Topic. Other extension activities highlight the case of the notorious Unabomber and have students carry out a small-scale research project on surveillance.

Connect to the Topic page 72   ~10 minutes

Students take a survey about their beliefs concerning safety and surveillance, comparing their responses with those of a partner. Encourage students to discuss any similarities and differences in their responses.

Build Your Vocabulary pages 73–74   ~15 minutes

Students study the following words and phrases related to political science and surveillance:

access to	deterrent	suspected of
aspect of	equivalent to	take advantage of
become part of	exposed to	techniques
civil liberties	monitored by	threats to society
commercial	security	unaware of
composite	sophisticated	via
controversial	suspected	

After the Interact with Vocabulary! activity, you may want to have students practice using the boldfaced words with their partners. Knowing collocations can help students expand their vocabularies and increase their fluency.

Focus Your Attention page 75   ~10 minutes

Students practice listening for and noting numbers and statistics. You may want to emphasize to students that sometimes the only way to distinguish two similar sounding words is by noticing their stress patterns. Also draw students' attention to any alternative ways of saying numbers and statistics (e.g., "two hundred *and* thirty-four" versus "two hundred thirty-four," etc.).

Listen to the Lecture pages 76–77   ~30 minutes

Students make a short list of ways that information can be gathered about people in their daily lives (Before You Listen) before listening to the unit lecture on surveillance. Students then answer sentence completion items (Listen for Main Ideas) and true/false items (Listen for Details).

Lecture video time: 7 min. 38 sec.   *Number of episodes: 8*

Talk about the Topic *page 78*   *~20 minutes*

Four students—May, Qiang, Yhinny, and Michael—discuss the lecture. Part A focuses on matching these students with ideas from the discussion. In Part B, your students work on these discussion strategies:

- Agreeing: "I would say so."
- Asking for clarification or confirmation: "She says something like, 'Orwellian.' What is that?"
- Trying to reach a consensus: "In general, we all agree that some surveillance is necessary, but not all surveillance is good?"

For Part C, students are encouraged to use the discussion strategies they've learned. They may use phrases from the student discussion and/or the Discussion Strategy box, or come up with their own. Keep in mind that some students may be reluctant to talk about their fears, while others may be very open about discussing them.
Student discussion video time: 1 min. 43 sec.

Review Your Notes *page 79*   *~15 minutes*

Students focus on reconstructing their notes, paying particular attention to numbers and statistics and explaining them to a partner.

Take the Unit Test *Teacher's Pack page 49*   *~15 minutes*

You may want to play the lecture again just before giving the test. Students answer standard test questions about the content of the lecture. Specifically, the test covers the following: people's attitude toward surveillance, coverage of the lecture, definition of Big Brother culture, number of cameras in the U.K., credit card crime, biometric facial recognition, the lecturer's opinions about surveillance and privacy, and the meaning of "open-ended."

Extend the Topic *pages 80–81*   *~30 minutes*

- Listening and Discussion: Students listen to a news report on the Unabomber, Theodore Kaczynski, and discuss their views on his actions and the motivation for them.
- Reading and Discussion: They then read and comment on the views of three professional people on the right to privacy.
- Research and Presentation: Students complete the unit by carrying out a surveillance-related research project which they present to their classmates.

Focus Your Attention:
Try It Out! *page 75*

Speaker: Now let's look at figures. A report by the New York Civil Liberties Union, entitled "Who's Watching?" claims that there were a total of 2,397 surveillance cameras in all of Manhattan ten years ago. And that now there are that many cameras in just one area: Greenwich Village and SoHo. Apparently, the cameras have been a highly effective crime-fighting tool, reducing crime in the area by more than a third. The Metropolitan Transportation Authority now plans to spend up to $250 million on cameras for the city's subway system. And the New York City Police Department has requested funding for about 400 digital video cameras to help combat robberies and burglaries. Additionally, it has received $9.8 million from the Federal Department of Homeland Security to help create a linked system of cameras that can be operated from a control center. Surveillance Camera Players—a New York City-based anti-camera group—is concerned by these developments. They've quoted camera growth-rates of 300, 500, and even 1,400 percent, depending on the neighborhood. Those are really substantial increases . . .

Listen for Main Ideas and Listen for Details *pages 76–77*

Political science lecturer: E1 One controversial aspect of civil liberties we've not touched on yet is surveillance. Let's start with a definition so we know what we're talking about: "Surveillance is the act of carefully watching a person or place, especially one that's suspected." Well, I'm sure we all have our own opinions on this. E2 Civil liberties groups in most countries are concerned that we're becoming a so-called "surveillance culture"—that in the name of national and personal security, national governments are obtaining detailed information on their citizens and tracking their movements, Internet use, financial transactions, and so on. And it's not just the government. Today it's possible for savvy private organizations to get information on individuals from different sources and build a kind of composite picture—a profile, if you will. Some people think that this is fine—if it helps the government, or if their local supermarket knows their shopping habits—they shouldn't have anything to hide, right? But most people don't like it. They feel they've become part of an Orwellian "Big Brother" culture—that it's a gross intrusion of privacy. E3 Are they right? Well, you can judge for

yourselves because I'm going to take you through some of the surveillance mechanisms that are out there. We'll start by looking at a few of the more familiar ones, and then move on to a more recent and technically sophisticated method. First up: Cameras. Today, these are everywhere: Closed-circuit TV cameras are in stores monitoring shoplifters, in cash machines identifying fraud gangs, and on public transport watching vandals and thugs. But of course, they're also watching perfectly ordinary, innocent people like you and me going about their daily lives completely unaware that they're being monitored. You know, today in the U.S. for example, there are probably upwards of 6 million surveillance cameras. In New York City alone, they've increased 50 percent in the past few years. And in Britain that figure is 4.5 million cameras. That's one camera for every fourteen people recording each citizen up to 300 times a day! Then there are traffic-based cameras monitoring vehicles via their registration numbers. Right now, the U.K. government is considering recording all car journeys taken on main roads as a deterrent to terrorism and crime generally. These cameras are being used way beyond their original purpose—it's downright invasive. E4 Cell phones have given the authorities another useful surveillance tool. Records of incoming and outgoing calls can be checked and used to solve crimes—that's right, just like in the movies! And—something I didn't know—cell phone users can be tracked using a system called triangulation. This is when a cell phone's communication with different cell phone towers is used to locate the user's position. And seeing as these days almost all of us have one of these phones, what's there to stop security services from checking on any one of us? E5 Then we have credit card transactions. We're all familiar with this one, I'm sure. Every time we use a credit or debit card, we're making an announcement of where we are, how much we're spending, and on what. Again, useful for crime-busting when, say, unusually large amounts of money are suddenly spent uncharacteristically. But do we really want people to know this stuff? Do we want anyone having access to our financial records? E6 OK, let's look at one of the more sophisticated surveillance techniques: biometric facial recognition, which uses computer programs to analyze images of human faces for identification purposes. And they do it by taking an image, say, from a photo or video frame, then they measure facial characteristics, like the distance between your eyes and the length of your nose, for instance. Then they create a template which the software can compare with another image, like of a person going through airport security. If there's a match, then, hey, presto, that person gets pulled aside for questioning. They've got this system operating at a number of airports. It's also been used at major sporting events like the Super Bowl, where pictures were taken of every person entering the stadium and then compared against a database. E7 Now, all the instances of surveillance I've mentioned are products of the digital age, of technology that's now so easily available that it's just too simple and tempting for security agencies and commercial organizations not to take advantage of it. And here's the catch: Just to function in today's world requires us, increasingly, to expose ourselves to these threats to our privacy. We basically have no choice. Let's face it, how many of us these days can really manage without a credit card, an ID card, e-mail, or a cell phone? It's almost as if, well, if we want to have these things, then we have to accept the surveillance that goes with them, right? E8 Now I'm no conspiracy theorist, but, like many people, I don't believe all this surveillance is for our own good. I don't believe that those of us who have nothing to hide have nothing to fear. So it's reassuring that there are organizations out there protecting the rights of ordinary citizens like you and me. Let me wrap up with a quote from Marc Rotenberg, President of the Electronic Privacy Information Center, or EPIC, who says that the kind of "open-ended surveillance" we are now seeing is, quote, "the digital electronic equivalent of allowing police to go through your home without a warrant." Now that's a sobering thought, wouldn't you say?

Coaching Tips

[1] **Listening: Listening for definitions** The speaker gives a definition of a key term. Did you hear it? Did you write it in your notes? Even if you don't get every word of the definition, the parts you do write down will help you to reconstruct the definition later. You can always consult a dictionary, a classmate, or the speaker to clarify your understanding of a term.

Find audioscript for the other Coaching Tips at www.pearsonlongman.com/contemporarytopics.

Talk about the Topic *page 78*

Michael: So this surveillance lecture was pretty controversial, huh?

Yhinny: Yeah, like she said at the end, "That's a sobering thought, wouldn't you say?"

Michael: Well, I don't think any of us would disagree with her. I mean, she said not all surveillance is for our own good. Right?

May: Yeah.

Qiang: Yeah.

Qiang: Yeah, but, I have a question. She says something like "Orwellian." What is that?

Yhinny: Orwellian. Yeah, she's talking about George Orwell. He wrote a book called *1984*. It's

about the surveillance society. In that book, they coined the expression, "Big Brother's watching you!"

May: Yeah, but I don't think it's that bad just yet. I think she's exaggerating a little bit. I don't think that "Big Brother" is watching over us all the time.

Michael: OK, maybe not all the time. But I mean, should there be some sort of limit to it? I mean, is it really all for our own good? Or for our own safety?

May: Uh-huh.

Yhinny: Well, like when I ride the subway at night, and I know that there's a video camera on on the train, I feel safer. So for me, I mean, it's fine with me.

May: Of course.

Qiang: Well, of course, some of it is useful. But a lot of it is intrusive. Like the traffic cameras that feed to the Internet site(s). Many of them can look into people's homes, and you can see everything.

Yhinny: Wow, so like everything about you can instantly be on the Internet?

Qiang: Yes.

Yhinny: Wow, that is totally wrong.

Michael: So, in general we all agree that some surveillance is necessary, but not all surveillance is good?

Yhinny: Yeah, I'd say so.

Qiang: Yeah, in a nutshell.

May: More or less, that's it. Uh-huh.

Michael: OK, so can we say that we're all on the same page for this?

Yhinny: I guess.

Michael: OK. Let's move on. What's next?

Take the Unit Test

1. How do most people feel about surveillance?
2. Which topics does the speaker *not* talk about? Choose *two* answers.
3. What does the speaker mean by a "Big Brother" culture?
4. Why does the speaker mention that there are 4.5 million cameras in the U.K.?
5. Why is the U.K. government considering recording all car journeys?
6. What can alert the authorities to credit card crime?
7. Which phrase best describes biometric facial recognition?
8. What is the speaker's opinion about threats to our privacy?
9. Which of these ideas would the speaker strongly support?
10. Marc Rotenberg describes surveillance today as "open-ended." What does he mean?

Extend the Topic *page 80*

Anchor: The man known as the "Unabomber" was sentenced today in Sacramento, California. Following a seventeen-year-long manhunt, Theodore Kaczynski, a graduate of Harvard and one-time Berkeley professor, received four life terms in prison plus an additional thirty years. Kaczynski sent bombs through the mail, killing three people and injuring twenty-nine others. He has acknowledged responsibility for sixteen bombings between 1978 and 1995. In what has become known as the "Unabomber Manifesto" —a document he named "Industrial Society and Its Future"—Kaczynski argued that his actions were a necessary, if extreme, tactic designed to draw attention to what he believes are the dangers of modern technology. His bombs targeted universities and airline companies—organizations he associated with the development and application of the kind of technology he resented. The Unabomber has been the target of one of the most expensive investigations in the FBI's history. And, of course, one of the most surprising aspects of the case is that the eventual breakthrough came when Kaczynski's own brother, David, provided the police with evidence strongly implicating Kaczynski. A plea bargain saved Kaczynski from a trial and a death sentence. With Kaczynski in prison, it's hoped that closure can be brought to what has been a drawn-out and frustrating case for police. Our next story concerns . . .

ANSWER KEY

Build Your Vocabulary *pages 73–74*

A. 1. rights, freedoms 2. business, trade 3. made, different parts 4. lot, disagreement 5. stopping, doing 6. measures, protect 7. advanced, complex 8. believed, responsible, wrong 9. methods, doing 10. through, by **C. Interact with Vocabulary!** 1. of 2. by 3. of 4. of 5. to 6. to 7. to 8. to 9. of 10. of

Focus Your Attention *page 75*

A. 2,397; 400; $9.8 million; 300%, 500%, 1,400%

Listen for Main Ideas *page 76*

B. 1. watching, suspected 2. government, organizations 3. invasion 4. three hundred 5. solve crimes 6. credit card 7. biometric facial recognition

Listen for Details *page 77*

B. 1. F (are becoming concerned about) 2. F ("surveillance cultures") 3. F (50%) 4. F (to track calls) 5. T 6. F (airports & sporting events) 7. T 8. F (appears to be concerned about)

Talk about the Topic *page 78*

A. 1. Michael 2. May 3. Yhinny 4. Qiang, Yhinny **B.** Agreeing: 4; Asking for clarification or confirmation: 1, 2; Trying to reach a consensus: 3

Review Your Notes *page 79*

Def.: carefully watching a person/place, especially one that's suspected; **Reasons concerned:** becoming "surveillance culture" w/gov'ts and org.'s obtaining detailed info on citizens, tracking movements, Internet use, fin'l transactions; **4 surveillance uses:** 1. monitoring $ machines, fraud gangs, vandals & thugs on pub. transport; 2. recording calls to solve crimes, tracking cell phone users; 3. ID'ing illeg. transactions, cc fraud & related criminal activities, people's location, $ habits; 4. analyzing images of faces for ID purposes; **the lecturer's view:** anti-surveillance; civil liberties orgs = reassuring; **Marc Rotenberg's view:** current level of surveillance ~ police going thru home w/o warrant

Take the Unit Test

1. b 2. a and d 3. c 4. c 5. c 6. c 7. a 8. c 9. b 10. b

UNIT 8 TEST POLITICAL SCIENCE: Big Brother and the Surveillance Society

 Listen to each question. Circle the letter of the correct answer.

1. a. They like it; it makes them feel safe.

   b. They dislike it.

   c. They feel they have nothing to fear if they've done nothing wrong.

   d. They think it's a necessary evil.

2. a. store loyalty cards

   b. cell phone triangulation

   c. traffic-based cameras

   d. phone tapping

3. a. a culture in which you have no freedom

   b. a technologically sophisticated culture

   c. a culture in which everything you do is watched by the authorities

   d. a culture in which surveillance is used widely to fight crime

4. a. to show that 1 in 14 people are being protected

   b. to explain how a single person is recorded up to 300 times a day

   c. as an example of how invasive cameras are

   d. to argue the need for more cameras in New York City

5. a. to identify illegal drivers

   b. to help stop speeding

   c. to deter terrorism

   d. to identify stolen cars

6. a. closed-circuit TV cameras in stores

   b. transactions made over cell phones

   c. the sudden spending of large amounts of money

   d. multiple withdrawals of cash in a short period of time

7. a. a computer program that compares an actual image with a template

   b. a computer program that draws people based on multiple descriptions

   c. a computerized videotaping technique

   d. a computer program designed to create digital photos of criminals from videos

8. a. They are not as great as many people believe.

   b. They are exaggerated by security agencies.

   c. They cannot be avoided in modern society.

   d. They can only be avoided by technology experts.

9. a. the surveillance of government officials

   b. the work of civil liberties organizations

   c. the limited use of cell phones by ordinary citizens

   d. the tracking of only suspicious people

10. a. Anybody is free to do it.

    b. There are no controls or limits on it.

    c. It will never be banned.

    d. It's a threat to everybody.

LINGUISTICS
Animal Communication

UNIT OVERVIEW

In this unit, students work with concepts related to the issue of animal communication and how it is both similar to and different from human language. The lecture focuses on four characteristics of human languages: arbitrariness (the lack of logical relationship between a sound and its meaning), displacement (the ability to communicate about things that are not physically present), cultural transmission (the ability to pass language from one generation to the next), and discreteness (the ability to combine discrete units in a language in many different ways).

Connect to the Topic *page 82*   *~10 minutes*

Students take a survey about their beliefs concerning animal communication. Survey questions include animals' ability to understand and express emotions, and their ability to use words. Students are asked to support their opinions with reasons or examples.

Build Your Vocabulary *pages 83–84*   *~15 minutes*

Students study the following words and phrases related to linguistics and animal communication:

accent	flexible	perceptions of
capacity for	generation	precise
communicate with	impressive	random
compared to	nonverbal behavior	refer to
convey information to	nothing arbitrary	skilled at
discrete	about	ultimately
distinct	number of	a wide range of

For the Interact with Vocabulary! activity, you may want to encourage students to first notice the boldfaced words. Figuring out these collocations can help students more quickly unscramble the sentences.

Focus Your Attention *page 85*   *~10 minutes*

Students learn the following cues, used by lecturers to compare and contrast ideas.

Comparisons	*in a similar manner*	*while*
like	*both . . . and . . .*	*more (than)*
in the same way	*parallels*	*whereas*
as . . . as	*in like fashion*	*different from*
also		*less (than)*
likewise	**Contrasts**	*on the other hand*
as with . . . so too with	*but*	*in contrast*
not only . . . but also	*however*	*unlike*
similar to/similarly	*conversely*	*although*

Listen to the Lecture *pages 86–87* ~30 minutes

Students think of and list three ways that animals communicate (Before You Listen) before listening to the unit lecture on animal communication. Students then answer multiple-choice items (Listen for Main Ideas) and sentence completion items (Listen for Details).
Lecture video time: 5 min. 52 sec.   *Number of episodes: 7*

Talk about the Topic *page 88* ~20 minutes

Four students—Hannah, River, Mia, and Manny—discuss the lecture. Part A focuses on matching these students with ideas from the discussion. In Part B, your students work on these discussion strategies:

- Expressing an opinion: "Personally, I think animal communication is a lot more sophisticated than we understand."
- Agreeing: "Pretty much."
- Asking for clarification or confirmation: "Is that what everyone else got from this lecture?"

For Part C, students are encouraged to use the discussion strategies they've learned. They may use phrases from the student discussion or come up with their own.
Student discussion video time: 1 min. 36 sec.

Review Your Notes *page 89* ~15 minutes

Students focus on reconstructing important information about the lecture, using the key words and phrases provided.

BONUS ACTIVITY

As a lead-in to the unit test, you can supplement this activity by asking students to make an original list of words and phrases from the lecture and to exchange lists with a classmate. Students should then create sentences orally or in writing using their classmate's list.

Take the Unit Test *Teacher's Pack page 55* ~15 minutes

You may want to play the lecture again just before giving the test. Students answer standard test questions about the content of the lecture. Specifically, the test covers the following: the main ideas of the lecture; the definition of displacement; the creatures that can use displacement, cultural transmission, and discreteness; chimpanzees' ability to use language; animals' ability to communicate about the past; and humans' ability to communicate with animals.

Extend the Topic *pages 90–91* ~30 minutes

- Listening and Discussion: Students listen to and discuss a researcher's thoughts on animal emotions.
- Reading and Discussion: Students read an article from the Internet about an animal whisperer and a skeptic, then discuss.
- Research and Presentation: Students research the communicative behavior of a specific animal and present their findings to the class.

Focus Your Attention: Try It Out! *page 85*

Speaker: OK, on a related note: Two common, but very different modes of animal communication are acoustic signals, or sounds, and chemical signals. Acoustic signals can travel long distances and do so almost instantly. These sounds can also be altered in useful ways. For instance, the pitch, loudness, and rhythm of a sound can be changed. This allows animals to communicate different meanings. Like acoustic signals, chemical signals can travel long distances, too. But they require much more time to do so because they depend on moving air or water. Similar to acoustic signals, chemical signals can be altered in many ways. For instance, a little bit of a chemical can attract other animals, while a greater amount of the same chemical can repel them. Chemical signals can also be used for marking territory and trails. . . .

Listen for Main Ideas and Listen for Details *pages 86–87*

Linguistics lecturer: E1 How many of you have pets? They're great, aren't they? I've got a golden retriever myself, and often I feel that my dog is communicating with me. But do animals really communicate like we do? Well, Harvard professor Marc Hauser has identified several types of animal communication. And like humans, they do use sounds and nonverbal behavior to communicate. For instance, they convey information to one another, they establish and maintain social organization, and they express their perceptions of the world. So today we'll look at animal communication through the lens of human language. Specifically, we'll use four basic characteristics of human language to see how animal and human communication styles compare. I think that you'll be surprised at how sophisticated animal communication is. But ultimately, we'll see that human communication is far more flexible and better developed. **E2** Now, the first characteristic we'll look at is arbitrariness. Arbitrariness means that there's no logical relationship between a sound and its meaning. For example, the word *sky* has no relationship with the thing it refers to, right? In comparison, a lot of animal communication is not arbitrary. For example, the growl of an angry dog is meant to very directly warn and threaten. There's nothing "arbitrary" about this message, right? However, some animal communication is arbitrary, albeit to a limited degree. For example, meerkats—a small African animal—can make about twenty distinct sounds. They use one alarm call for snakes, another for eagles, and yet another for large cats, just to name a few, OK? **E3** This is impressive. But human languages are far more flexible because they have a wide range of sounds. English, for example, has more than forty distinct sounds such as /a/, /k/, or /t/. And we can make an unlimited number of arbitrary words by altering these sounds—far more than any animal. **E4** The second characteristic of human language we'll compare is displacement. Displacement is communicating ideas about things that are not physically present. For example, if you talk about what you did last weekend, that's displacement. Now, can animals do this? Well, often the answer is they can't. For instance, if your dog doesn't like the neighbor cat, maybe it barks when it sees the cat. But when the cat isn't around, the dog doesn't bark—it doesn't communicate its dislike of the cat. This shows that the dog doesn't have the capacity for displacement. **E5** Well, one exception to this is bees. Many types of bees use displacement in their dances. Through these dances, they're able to communicate to other bees the distance, direction, quality, and quantity of a food source. The meaning of the dance is so clear and so precise that even scientists researching bee dances can interpret exactly where the food is. In any case, although I think that the bees is an excellent example of the sophistication of animal communication, in general, animals' use of displacement is extremely limited compared to humans. Think about books, magazines, and the Internet. I mean, everything that we read involves displacement, as do most of our conversations. **E6** The third characteristic of human language that I want to consider is called cultural transmission, the idea that language is passed from one generation to the next. Now, obviously, humans excel at this, but what about animals? Well, some animals are also fairly skilled at passing language on to their young. A good example of this is the killer whale. They live in groups, and different groups develop different accents, just like people. The accents are passed from older to younger killer whales. Well, this is yet another example of the sophistication of some animal communication. However, once again, what we see is that while animal and human communication share similarities, the characteristics that we are looking for are far more developed in humans. For example, in addition to accents, humans also pass on extremely large vocabularies and complex grammar. **E7** The fourth and last characteristic that we'll talk about today is called discreteness. This means that language is made up of discrete units that can be combined in different ways to create different meanings. As humans, we do this by using sounds to make words and using grammar to arrange those words into sentences. The best example we have of animals using discreteness is from chimpanzees raised in captivity. Using a keyboard, chimps have made requests for food by typing "raisin peanut," which seemed to mean "raisins and peanuts." Chimps have also invented phrases to describe things. For example, one chimp called watermelon, "drink fruit." Clever, huh? But while this is fairly impressive, one major problem with the chimpanzees' use of language is that their word order is quite random. So most linguists would say that the chimpanzees really do not understand and use grammar in the way that humans do, and therefore can't be said to use discreteness. In the use of discreteness, we see that humans have a huge advantage over animals. Discreteness allows us to make complex words and sentences that communicate an unlimited number of meanings, and this is one of the really impressive—actually amazing—aspects of human communication.

Coaching Tips

[1] Listening: Recognizing irrelevant details Why do you think the speaker asks students about their pets? And tells about his? By asking and sharing personal information, the speaker is helping his listeners warm up to the topic. That said, while this personal information may be interesting, the details often aren't relevant to the lecture. Therefore, it's not necessary to write it in your notes.

Find audioscript for the other Coaching Tips at www.pearsonlongman.com/contemporarytopics.

Talk about the Topic *page 88*

River: So, here's the lecture in a nutshell: Animals communicate. And they share some communication characteristics with us. But animal communication is less developed. Is that what everyone else got from this lecture?

Mia: Pretty much.

Hannah: Uh-huh.

Manny: Well, I agree that's what he said. But personally, I think animal communication is a lot more sophisticated than we understand.

Mia: How so? You really think it's as sophisticated as human communication?

Manny: In some ways, yeah. I mean, I saw this documentary about monkeys that give signals for, you know, birds, snakes, other animals—depending on what they see.

River: Yeah, but remember, that's not using, what was it? Arbitrariness. And it's not using displacement. Those are very clear and very present signals, right?

Mia: What is a meerkat, by the way?

Hannah: Oh, it's a kind of little monkey, or kind of like a cat, really. Looks like a raccoon, to me. Lives in Africa.

Mia: So, even though animal communication is kind of sophisticated, there seem to be very few examples of complex communication. Human communication is usually really complex, right?

Hannah: Yeah, like when you seem to be saying different things and therefore "send mixed signals."

Manny: Or when you're being very indirect and the other person has to "read between the lines."

Mia: Or what about when people are being like passive aggressive and saying one thing . . .

Hannah: I hate that!

Mia: . . . but really meaning something else.

River: That's like sending mixed signals and having to read between the lines.

Take the Unit Test

1. What is one of the main ideas of the lecture?
2. Which idea was *not* discussed in the lecture?
3. What is the definition of *displacement*?
4. Which creature can skillfully use displacement?
5. What sophisticated communication ability do killer whales possess?
6. What animal has shown a limited ability to use discreteness?
7. What are chimpanzees unable to do when they communicate?
8. Which of the following is probably true of animal communication?
9. What would the speaker probably say about animals' ability to communicate about past events?
10. What would the speaker probably say about humans' ability to communicate with animals?

Extend the Topic *page 90*

Journalist: So what would animals communicate about anyway? I mean, ideas? Feelings?

Researcher: Well, since there's still no convincing evidence that animals are capable of complex reasoning, we believe they're often communicating their feelings—what you and I would call emotions.

Journalist: Wow, such as happiness, sadness, anger?

Researcher: Well, we're not sure that animals experience the same emotions as you and I. But some of their feelings are probably similar. For instance, emotions like fear arise in a place in our brain that we share with many animals. So fear might feel similar for humans and animals. Another example is that some animals, such as dogs and elephants, seem to find joy in meeting friends and family. But we don't yet know just how similar their feelings are to our own.

Journalist: Right. Because animals can't tell us what they're feeling.

Researcher: True. One interesting idea is that animals experience emotions in a very pure way because their brain is less complex. For instance, when they feel joy, it may be a kind of pure, 100 percent joy, not a feeling like "I'm happy but . . . "

Journalist: Ah, I see. No "buts" for animals.

Researcher: Right. And if you think about it, this is how we experienced emotions when we were

small children. When we were happy, we were 100 percent happy. So maybe before our brain develops fully, we experience feelings that are similar to some animals.

Journalist: In that case, I'd have to say that I'm a bit envious of our animal friends. Who wouldn't want to feel 100 percent happiness? . . .

ANSWER KEY

Build Your Vocabulary *pages 83–84*
B. 1. d 2. b 3. f 4. g 5. e 6. h 7. a 8. j 9. i 10. c
C. 1. N 2. A 3. A 4. A 5. N 6. A 7. N 8. A 9. A
10. A **D. Interact with Vocabulary!** 1. believe that they can communicate with 2. can convey sophisticated information to one another 3. their perceptions of the world 4. do not refer to past events 5. nothing arbitrary about the meaning 6. use a wide range of 7. an unlimited number of sentences 8. have the capacity for using grammar 9. very limited when compared to 10. are skilled at acquiring the accent

Focus Your Attention *page 85*

	Acoustic signals	Chemical signals
distance of travel?	long	long
speed of travel?	instantly	more slowly (via air/water)
can be altered?	✓	✓
can be used for marking?		✓

Listen for Main Ideas *pages 86–87*
B. 1. a 2. b 3. a 4. c 5. c 6. b 7. a

Listen for Details *page 87*
B. 1. arbitrary 2. distinct meanings 3. sounds
4. displacement 5. scientists 6. sophistication
7. accents 8. phrases 9. grammar 10. discreteness

Talk about the Topic *page 88*
A. 1. Hannah, River, Mia 2. Manny 3. River
4. Hannah **B.** Expressing an opinion: 3; Agreeing:
2; Asking for clarification or confirmation: 1, 4

Review Your Notes *page 89*
Sample sentences: People communicate using verbal and nonverbal behavior involving the use of sounds.
Arbitrariness means that there's no logical relationship between a sound and its meaning.
Humans' ability to communicate is flexible because we can use a wide range of sounds.
Bees use displacement when they communicate about food sources that are not physically present.
Humans use displacement every time they read books or use the Internet.
Killer whales use cultural transmission when they pass accents on to the next generation.
Chimpanzees use discreteness when they combine words to make new phrases.
Humans use discreteness when they combine words to make grammar.

Take the Unit Test
1. b 2. d 3. b 4. a 5. c 6. c 7. d 8. c 9. c 10. b

UNIT 9 TEST LINGUISTICS: Animal Communication

 Listen to each question. Circle the letter of the correct answer.

1. a. Animal communication has evolved from simple to complex forms.
   b. Animal communication is less sophisticated than human language.
   c. Animals possess large vocabularies but little syntax.
   d. Animals communicate complex ideas, but only with their own species.

2. a. humans' frequent use of arbitrariness
   b. animals' inability to use syntax
   c. animals' use of cultural transmission
   d. animals' use of language to bond with humans

3. a. the lack of a relationship between a sound and its meaning
   b. communicating ideas about things that are not physically present
   c. the ability to pass information on to the next generation
   d. the ability to use complex grammar

4. a. bees
   b. chimpanzees
   c. dogs
   d. meerkats

5. a. nonverbal communication
   b. a large vocabulary
   c. cultural transmission
   d. complex grammar

6. a. bees
   b. cats
   c. chimpanzees
   d. killer whales

7. a. learn words
   b. use nonverbal communication
   c. communicate the location of food sources
   d. understand and use grammar

8. a. Animals mostly use language to communicate with different species.
   b. Animal language is as sophisticated as human language.
   c. Animal language differs from human language in many ways.
   d. Animals mostly rely on verbal communication.

9. a. It is not possible.
   b. Only chimpanzees can do it.
   c. Bees and their dances provide the closest example of this.
   d. Many animals can do it.

10. a. It is not impossible.
    b. It is possible, but only to a limited degree.
    c. Animals must first learn to use grammar.
    d. Animals must first learn to pronounce a human language.

UNIT 10 ECONOMICS
The Evolution of Money

UNIT OVERVIEW

In this unit, students learn about the benefits that money has produced for society and how money has evolved from one form to another. The first part of the lecture focuses on four advantages of money over barter: transactions of any size can take place, transactions can be completed extremely quickly, transactions can take place across cultural and geographic boundaries, and the value of money is precise and consistent. The second part of the lecture outlines money's evolution from a physical object to an abstract idea. Follow-up projects extend the topic to topics such as the future of money and the extremes of wealth and poverty found in the world today.

Connect to the Topic *page 92*   *~10 minutes*

Students take a survey about their attitudes toward money. Survey questions concern issues such as personal finance and the importance of money for both individuals and society.

Build Your Vocabulary *pages 93–94*

Students study the following words and phrases related to economics and money:

abandoned	enormous	played a role in
abstract	facilitator of	subjective
at this stage	fluctuations in	symbolic of
carry out	heredity	tied to
civilization	initiative	transactions
currency	move away	undergone
development of	from	

For the Interact with Vocabulary! activity, you may want to encourage students to first notice the boldfaced words. Figuring out these collocations can help students more quickly unscramble the sentences.

Focus Your Attention *page 95*   *~10 minutes*

Students learn these strategies to help them think more deeply about the information in their notes:

Underline important ideas.	Draw lines to show relationships.
Draw stars to show the most important ideas.	Write comments in the margins.
	Write questions in the margins.
Circle key words and phrases.	Write a summary statement.

Listen to the Lecture *pages 96–97*   *~30 minutes*

Students consider the flexibility and influences of money (Before You Listen) before listening to the unit lecture on the benefits and evolution of money. Students then answer true/false items (Listen for Main Ideas) and sentence completion items (Listen for Details).
Lecture video time: 6 min. 35 sec.   Number of episodes: 8

Talk about the Topic   *page 98*   *~20 minutes*

Four students—Ayman, Molly, Rob, and Alana—discuss the lecture. Part A focuses on matching these students with comments from the discussion. In Part B, your students work on these discussion strategies:

- Expressing an opinion: "It's kind of cool to think that we're seeing money's latest evolution."
- Agreeing: "I don't blame you . . . "
- Offering a fact or example: "My credit card number got stolen sometime last weekend."

For Part C, students are encouraged to use the discussion strategies they've learned. They may use phrases from the student discussion and/or the Discussion Strategy box, or come up with their own. Keep in mind that students should provide reasons for their answers and elaborate on their responses.
Student discussion video time: 1 min. 30 sec.

Review Your Notes   *page 99*   *~15 minutes*

Students focus on reconstructing their notes, paying attention to giving examples and adding their own comments.

BONUS ACTIVITY

As a lead-in to the unit test, you can supplement this activity by asking students to select five words or phrases that they think are particularly important in this lecture. They should then work with a partner to define and give examples of each one.

Take the Unit Test   *Teacher's Pack page 61*   *~15 minutes*

You may want to play the lecture again just before giving the test. Students answer standard test questions about the content of the lecture. Specifically, the test covers the following: the definition of barter, the main points of the lecture, the advantages of money over barter, forms that money has taken, digital money, and the lecturer's attitude toward money.

Extend the Topic   *pages 100–101*   *~30 minutes*

- Listening and Discussion: Students listen to and discuss an economist's ideas on the future of money.
- Reading and Discussion: Students read statistics on wealth and poverty around the world, then discuss.
- Research and Presentation: Students research and present on how something other than money has changed and how it might look in the future.

Focus Your Attention:
Try It Out! *page 95*

Speaker: OK, let's move on. At present, fewer than 200 currencies are in use in the world. But will that be true thirty or forty years from now? Probably not. In the near future, a few regional currency blocs will probably develop. Europe has already done this with the euro. In the near future, we may see a North American bloc, an Asian bloc, and a South American bloc develop. In thirty years, we may have fewer than ten currencies in the world. And then given a bit more time, those currencies may merge into a single world currency. Why would this happen? First of all, a single currency would eliminate destructive currency fluctuations, or when the currency of a single country loses value suddenly. Secondly, trade between countries would be far easier and less expensive. Thirdly, there would be no need for countries to keep reserves of other countries' money because they would all be using the same currency. Countries could use the money that had been kept in reserve in far more productive ways . . .

Listen for Main Ideas and Listen for Details *pages 96–97*

Economics lecturer: E1 Money. It's one of the greatest creations of human history and has played a positive role in the development of modern civilization. However, we haven't always used money. If we look back, say, more than 3,000 years ago, which is when coins first appeared, we would find that most people conducted business using a system of direct exchange called barter. For instance, I might exchange my five chickens for your three sheep. That's barter. Today I'll be talking about some advantages of money over barter, how money has undergone change over time, and the benefits of money. E2 OK, in early societies, land and agriculture provided the main forms of wealth and power. How? Because only landowners could grow large amounts of food and raise large amounts of animals, such as cattle and sheep. Although people could carry out limited business transactions by bartering animals and vegetables, the barter system was doomed to fail. Why? E3 Well, you'll see through the four enormous advantages of money I'm about to explain. The first advantage is that financial transactions of any size can take place—an advantage that increased tremendously when paper money was introduced. For example, it's simple for a company to make a transaction involving millions

or billions of dollars when using money. Second, transactions involving money can be done fast. People who have money can get it and transfer it to another person rapidly. This means that business can be conducted quickly. And now of course, with electronic transactions, money can be moved over any distance in a flash. Third, money allows people to do business with anyone, across cultural or geographic boundaries, and this greatly expands business opportunities. Money truly enjoys universal acceptance. The fourth advantage is that the value of money is precise and consistent. Precise means that the value of money can be determined in exact ways—$5.49 or $5.51. Money is also consistent because the value of one dollar is one dollar—it isn't subjective. And even when the value of a currency fluctuates, it fluctuates for everyone. E4 OK, let me say a few words about the evolution of money. Originally, money was a physical object found in nature—cattle and grains, for example. It then evolved to become a manufactured physical object, such as gold and silver coins. Next, money became something more abstract, something that is symbolic of physical objects such as gold and silver. At this stage in its evolution, money became pieces of paper, such as paper money and stock certificates. While gold and silver coins have real value, paper doesn't, because it's completely separated from what it once represented—gold. This was an enormous evolutionary leap because money moved from being a concrete, physical object to being a symbolic, abstract idea. And this idea worked only because people had a great deal of trust and faith in the principle. E5 OK, now what about the benefits that have resulted from the invention of money? I'll cover three. The invention has benefited commerce, human initiative, and individual freedom. Traditionally, wealth was handed down from parent to child in the form of land. And because few people were landowners, few people had any hope of advancing in society or of becoming even moderately wealthy. However, as agriculture became increasingly efficient, more and more people abandoned farmwork. These people began to live in cities and to make their livings by offering non-agricultural products and services. Money was the facilitator of this commerce because, as we just saw, money allows businesspeople to sell goods to anyone, right? E6 Second point—the rise of commerce increased individual initiative because wealth was no longer necessarily tied to heredity. Instead, brains and hard work became important. The result? Growing middle class and upper classes of relatively wealthy people. E7 And thirdly, people working in non-agricultural businesses gained the freedom to choose their own futures. For example, education became accessible to many more people. As a result, they were better able to function independently and successfully. This further accelerated the growth of both new businesses and money. Can you see that? E8 All right, to sum up, money is one of the greatest and most productive tools ever created by human beings. It's a tool that's strongly related to human and social development, to creativity, and frankly, to turning dreams into reality. But the true source of all of these benefits is not money itself, because money is just an abstraction. Humans are the ones who give meaning to money, and through this very human use of trust and faith, millions of people have been able to live better, more comfortable, and more fulfilling lives.

Coaching Tips

[1] **Listening: Identifying main ideas** At the beginning of a lecture, most speakers will use an attention-getting technique. They may tell a story, list some facts, or provide historical background. Listening carefully to the introduction a) gives you a glimpse of the "big picture" and b) highlights the main points to be covered. Here, try focusing on just listening to the speaker's introduction without taking notes. This way, you'll have a clear idea of where she's going with the lecture, and you can organize your notes accordingly.

Find audioscript for the other Coaching Tips at www.pearsonlongman.com/contemporarytopics.

Talk about the Topic *page 98*

Rob: I think all the different concepts involved are neat. It's, it's fun to play around with the different ideas behind it all.

Ayman: Yeah, yeah. It's kind of cool to think that we're seeing money's latest evolution. Like she said, we've gone from cows to gold to paper and now, electronic money.

Molly: Yeah, well, actually, based on my recent luck, I'd like to make a case for going back to cows.

Alana: Why?

Molly: Oh, my credit card number got stolen sometime last weekend, and now, I have all these crazy charges on my account.

Rob: What happened? Did you lose your card or something?

Molly: No. I mean, it actually, it never left my purse. But, somehow somebody got a hold of the account number and the password, and they bought, you know, online jewelry and these really expensive boots in Berlin and then CDs in London.

Alana: How'd you find this out?

Molly: Actually, the credit card company called me, you know, they wanted to verify some of the charges. They thought it was suspicious that there were charges made in the U.S. and Germany and England all in the same day.

Rob: Wow. Well, it's good that they found it so fast, though.

Molly: Yeah.

Ayman: So, did you have to pay for anything?

Molly: No, fortunately the credit card company's covering it all—I mean, that's their policy when there's theft or fraud. But, the whole episode's just kind of bummed me out, you know? I mean, I think I'm just going to stick to cash right now—and I don't really trust electronic money.

Alana: I don't blame you, but cash is risky, too. You know, you could get robbed.

Molly: Thank you for the comforting thought!

Rob: Yeah, what are you trying to do to her over there?

Molly: Yeah!

Rob: That's scary though about the credit card numbers.

Molly: I know.

Rob: And to think that you had the thing the whole time.

Molly: I know.

Take the Unit Test

1. What is exchanging five chickens for two sheep an example of?
2. What is one of the main points of the lecture?
3. Which of the following topics was *not* discussed in the lecture?
4. Why was wealth possessed by landowners in early societies?
5. Which of the following is *not* an advantage of money?
6. What was the earliest form of money?
7. What was one result of greater agricultural efficiency?
8. Which of the following ideas about money is probably true?
9. What does the speaker probably think about new digital forms of money?
10. What is the speaker's attitude toward money?

Extend the Topic *page 100*

Gray: Mika, thanks for joining us to talk about the future of money. So what does the future hold for us?

Mika: Well, Gray, I can sum it up in three words: *digital, virtual,* and *universal.*

Gray: OK. Let's take those one at a time. So how about *digital*?

Mika: The use of credit and debit cards will continue to grow, and eventually we'll reach a place where cash—coins and paper money—will be a thing of the past. Although the credit and debit cards qualify as digital money, they aren't virtual because they're still physical objects.

Gray: And what would qualify as *virtual* money?

Mika: In the future, touch-screen interfaces will be absolutely everywhere—in every home and every store. When we want to buy something, the system will identify us by our voice, fingerprint, or face. We'll then type in information about the transaction and make our purchase. No cash, no credit card, nothing physical. The transaction will take place completely over computer networks—that's virtual.

Gray: Interesting. And how about the last one? *Universal?*

Mika: *Universal* means that we'll eventually use a single, digital currency. Not dollars, euros, or yen—the ones and zeroes found in computer code will become the world currency. Although some national governments will resist the move away from having a national currency, having a universal currency will stimulate the world economy in ways that are difficult to imagine at present.

Gray: OK. There you have it. *Digital, virtual, universal.* Thanks so much for being with us today.

ANSWER KEY

Build Your Vocabulary   *pages 93–94*

A. 1. b 2. a 3. c 4. c 5. c 6. b 7. a 8. b 9. a 10. b
B. Interact with Vocabulary! 1. Money has played a positive role in 2. at this stage of its evolution 3. Fluctuations in currency values 4. is symbolic of valuable objects 5. has acted as a facilitator of business 6. almost exclusively tied to heredity. 7. to move away from 8. to carry out business with one another 9. to the development of modern societies

Focus Your Attention   *page 95*

A. *Sample notes:* currently: ~ <u>200</u> currencies
near future: regional currency blocks will appear (e.g., the euro)
in 30 yrs: maybe > ⑩ currencies & eventually a <u>single world currency</u>
*Reasons for a single currency:
eliminate currency fluctuations int'l trade
would be easier and ↓ $$$
no need to keep reserves of other countries' money

Listen for Main Ideas   *page 96*

B. 1. T 2. T 3. T 4. F (can) 5. F (does) 6. F (always) 7. T 8. T 9. F (because of, not independent of)

Listen for Details   *page 97*

B. 1. electronic transactions 2. precise 3. physical object 4. manufactured 5. paper money 6. agriculture 7. brains, working hard 8. education 9. social development 10. more fulfilling

Talk about the Topic   *page 98*

A. 1. Molly 2. Molly 3. Molly **B.** Expressing an opinion: 1, 3; Agreeing: 4; Offering a fact or example: 2

Review Your Notes   *page 99*

Def.: exchanging things of = value; **4 advantages:** (1) $ transaction of any size can take place, (2) transactions can be completed quickly (3) people can do business w/anyone (4) the value of $ is precise/consistent **3 benefits:** (1) commerce expanded greatly (2) human initiative ↑ (3) individual freedom ↑ **Evolution:** $ evolved from physical object in nature (~cows) to a manuf'd object (~gold coins) to ~paper money

Take the Unit Test

1. a 2. c 3. a 4. d 5. c 6. a 7. b 8. b 9. c 10. c

UNIT 10 TEST ECONOMICS: The Evolution of Money

Listen to each question. Circle the letter of the correct answer.

1. a. barter
   b. monetary precision
   c. a monetary transaction
   d. an abstract type of money

2. a. The main purpose of barter is human interaction.
   b. Wealth is not evenly distributed among nations.
   c. Money has evolved from physical to abstract forms.
   d. Financial transactions are increasing every year.

3. a. the benefits of the barter system
   b. the advantages of money over barter
   c. the ways in which money has changed
   d. the benefits of money

4. a. because landowners had access to gold and silver
   b. because landowners had access to natural resources in forests
   c. because landowners usually had large families
   d. because landowners could grow food and raise animals

5. a. Transactions of any size can take place.
   b. Transactions can take place quickly.
   c. The value of money constantly fluctuates.
   d. The value of money is precise.

6. a. natural physical objects such as grains
   b. valuable metals such as silver coins
   c. paper money
   d. digital money

7. a. The amount of food available to the average person increased sharply.
   b. People moved to cities and created non-agricultural products and services.
   c. Business transaction between neighboring countries increased.
   d. The average lifespan increased rapidly.

8. a. Barter had a limited number of advantages over money.
   b. Individual freedom underlies the creation of prosperous societies.
   c. Problems have arisen as money has become more abstract.
   d. Wealth has been used for the good of society throughout history.

9. a. They will cause unsolvable problems.
   b. They will soon disappear.
   c. They are part of money's evolution.
   d. They will decrease international trade.

10. a. She is suspicious of its effects on society.
    b. She feels jealous of those who have it.
    c. She is impressed by its changes over time.
    d. She is angry about the harm it has caused.

TEACHING TIPS

UNIT OVERVIEW

In this unit, students consider reasons for aging and ways to slow the aging process. The lecture focuses on two major theories of aging: program theories and damage theories. After considering why we age, the lecturer considers ways to slow the aging process, such as calorie restriction, slowing the metabolic rate, the use of stem cells, and a high-nutrition/low-calorie diet. Follow-up projects extend the topic to the impact of a positive outlook on aging, profiles of three centenarians, and research into other life-extension options.

Connect to the Topic *page 102*   *~10 minutes*

As a warm-up activity, consider having students look at the photos and share what they know about genetics and aging. In the survey that follows, students list advantages and disadvantages to aging, and then discuss their ideas.

Build Your Vocabulary *pages 103–104*   *~15 minutes*

Students study the following words and phrases related to biology and aging:

accelerate	caloric intake	metabolism
accelerated	calories	molecules
acceleration	cells	negative impact
accumulate	consistent with	nutrients
accumulating	electrons	nutrition
accumulation	function	nutritious
affected by	have the potential to	plus
benefit	interpretation of	supplement
biologists		

For the Interact with Vocabulary! activity, you may want to encourage students to first notice the boldfaced words. Understanding these collocations can help students more easily complete the sentences.

Focus Your Attention *page 105*   *~10 minutes*

Students learn cues that lecturers use when describing problems and possible solutions to those problems.

Expressing problems:	**Expressing reasons for problems:**	**Expressing solutions:**
The first problem is . . .	*The first reason is . . .*	*What can be done about this?*
The bad news is . . .	*A second major reason is . . .*	*How can we solve this problem?*
This causes problems such as . . .	*This is caused by . . .*	*There is some good news here . . .*
One theory of (the problem) says . . .	*This, in turn, causes . . .*	*Is there any good news here?*
Think about the implication . . .	*This happens because . . .*	*One possible solution is . . .*
	One interpretation is . . .	

Listen to the Lecture *pages 106–107*   *~30 minutes*

Students guess the top two causes of aging and two ways to slow aging (Before You Listen) before listening to the unit lecture on the causes of aging. Students then answer sentence completion items (Listen for Main Ideas) and multiple-choice items (Listen for Details).
Lecture video time: 6 min. 36 sec.   *Number of episodes: 7*

Talk about the Topic *page 108*   *~20 minutes*

Four students—Hannah, Manny, River, and Mia—discuss the lecture. Part A focuses on matching these students with opinions from the discussion. In Part B, your students work on these discussion strategies:

- Asking for opinions or ideas: "So what then?"
- Disagreeing: "I'm not so sure about that."
- Asking for clarification or confirmation: "Can I clarify something from earlier in the lecture?"

For Part C, students are encouraged to use the discussion strategies they've learned. They may use phrases from the student discussion and/or the Discussion Strategy box, or come up with their own.
Student discussion video time: 1 min. 38 sec.

Review Your Notes *page 109*   *~15 minutes*

Students focus on using their notes to complete a chart detailing the main ideas covered in the lecture.

BONUS ACTIVITY

As a lead-in to the unit test, you can ask students to write three quiz questions about the lecture that they can ask other students in the class.

Take the Unit Test *Teacher's Pack page 67*   *~15 minutes*

You may want to play the lecture again just before giving the test. Students answer standard test questions about the content of the lecture. Specifically, the test covers the following: the main topic of the lecture, the Hayflick Limit theory, the effects of reducing cellular waste, the effects of free radicals, the effects of reducing free radicals, and an anti-aging diet.

Extend the Topic *pages 110–111*   *~30 minutes*

- Listening and Discussion: Students listen to and discuss an excerpt about the impact of a positive outlook on aging.
- Reading and Discussion: Students read about and discuss living past 100 years old.
- Research and Presentation: Students research and present on other ways to extend life.

Focus Your Attention: Try It Out! *page 105*

Speaker: So, on to indicators of aging. The condition of our skin is one obvious indicator of aging. One reason that our skin ages prematurely is because of overeating foods such as meat, soft drinks, and sweets. These foods are associated with problems such as wrinkling. So what can be done about this? Well, for one, you can switch your diet to foods like olive oil, fish, eggs, vegetables, and fruit. All of these foods are associated with healthier skin. A second major reason that our skin ages is exposure to direct sunlight. The key to solving this problem is to avoid spending a lot of time outside between 10:00 A.M. and 4:00 P.M. And when you are outside, use a sunscreen that protects against UVA and UVB rays. It's also a good idea to get in the habit of wearing a hat. With a good diet and limited exposure to the sun, you can keep nice looking skin for many years to come. . . .

Listen for Main Ideas and Listen for Details *pages 106–107*

Biology lecturer: E1 OK, today I'd like to look at some theories of aging. Many theories of aging have been suggested, but most of them fall into just two categories: program theories and damage theories. Program theories say that our bodies are programmed to live for a limited amount of time, that information about our lifespan is encoded in our DNA. Damage theories, however, believe that damage to our cells is responsible for aging. Some early damage theories were based on the idea that the human body is mechanical, like a car, so it naturally breaks down over time. Now that is true to some extent, but unlike cars, our body has the capacity to heal and repair itself. E2 So, let's look at these two theories about aging, and along with that, consider some approaches to life extension. OK, let's first look at a program theory, the Hayflick Limit theory. This theory was proposed in the 1960s by two biologists who discovered that some cells divide about fifty times, then suddenly stop dividing. These were like lung, muscle, and heart cells, for example. In other words, after about fifty generations of cell division, which takes place over many years, the DNA just stops functioning. One interpretation of this is that a cellular clock is at work—that your time alive is genetically predestined. Now, this sounds like bad news, right? But there is some good news here. And here it is: The rate of cell division is directly affected by the amount of waste products in the cell. OK? So if we reduce the amount of waste, then the cells will divide more slowly. This means we can slow the hands of the clock and live longer. E3 So how do we reduce cellular waste? Well, some scientists think that they've found an effective way to do this: Eat less. About 30 percent less. It's called calorie restriction, or C-R. You cut out foods high in calories and low in nutrition—like those desserts we all love. And replace them with foods that are high in nutrition and low in calories—like fresh vegetables, for example. Currently, CR is the only known way to consistently increase lifespan. It's actually been shown to work well in dogs and monkeys. Also, CR doesn't just slow cell division, it lowers metabolic rate. Now this is potentially important because in mammals, lower metabolic rates are associated with longer life spans. So, listen carefully: The benefits of CR are twofold, right? One: slower cell division. And two: slower metabolism. Both of these can offer life extension. E4 However, let's think about the implications of a CR diet for a moment. Like, what economic impact would it have on the one-million-plus restaurants in the U.S. After all, they generate $500 billion annually. Or what about the people who earn a living on their physical strength? Could they function effectively on a CR diet? E5 OK, a second theory of aging—and this is a damage theory—states that our cells accumulate free radical damage with the passage of time. Now, what are free radicals? They're molecules in our body that have an extra electron. In normal molecules, electrons are paired, so that their electrical energies are balanced. But free radicals have an extra negative charge, and this causes them to attach to other molecules and cause an imbalance. They're caused by environmental factors that concern oxygen intake—air pollution and cigarette smoke, for example. And not only do they damage a cell's membrane and DNA, but they also make it more difficult for cells to repair the damage. This, in turn, causes aging to accelerate. E6 So is there any good news here? Is there any way to reduce the number of free radicals? Yes, and the key is oxygen. We know that animals with lower metabolic rates metabolize less oxygen. And less metabolized oxygen means a lower production of free radicals. Which means less cell damage. Make sense? So note that this is a second benefit of a lower metabolic rate. E7 So, scientists have learned in the last few decades a lot about why we age, but what can we do about it? Well, on one side, we have what might be called high-tech approaches, for example, the use of stem cells to act as a repair system for part of the body. Another approach is xenotransplantations, which uses animal tissues and organs to treat human beings. But both these approaches are controversial. On the other side, we have the natural approach, which is the approach I personally subscribe to. It's based on three common-sense ideas. First, eat a high-nutrition, low-calorie diet. That means lots of fruits and vegetables. Second, don't overeat—or as I mentioned before, reduce your intake of calories by about 30 percent. Third, supplement good eating with moderate exercise. Basically, the high-tech approach becomes unnecessary if we just apply this more natural approach.

Coaching Tips

[1] **Critical Thinking: Guessing** As the speaker explains, cellular waste in the cell contributes to aging, according to the Hayflick Limit theory. How do you think we can reduce cellular waste? Can you take a guess? We make guesses based on what we know, but of course our guesses aren't always correct. That's OK. Guessing will help you to prepare to hear and understand the information the speaker is about to give.

Find audioscript for the other Coaching Tips at www.pearsonlongman.com/contemporarytopics.

Talk about the Topic *page 108*

Mia: Really? Why not?

River: Well, I was really disappointed that she finished by talking about the "natural approach."

Mia: Huh?

River: You know, how if we use the natural approach to slow down aging, we don't have to use any high-tech solutions.

Mia: OK . . . ?

River: Well, taking the "natural approach" just seems like common sense. I mean, everybody knows that.

Hannah: I'm not so sure about that. I don't think it's common knowledge at all. I mean, that part about overeating having a connection to aging was news to me, and I consider myself pretty well informed.

Manny: Actually, I think people already know what they *should* do. But like me, they just don't.

River: Why's that?

Manny: Well, in my case, I don't have the time or the money to eat a super healthy diet. And I'm definitely not going to cut it back by 30 percent. I'd be hungry all the time!

Hannah: So what then? I mean, if you don't live a healthy lifestyle, your body will just break down faster, and you'll have to get a new heart some day.

Mia: Sorry to change the subject, but, can I clarify something from earlier in the lecture?

Hannah: Uh-huh.

Mia: So, has the Hayflick Limit theory been disproved? I'm talking about the interpretation that your lifespan is predestined.

Manny: By "predestined" do you mean . . . ?

Mia: Already decided. Like, the idea that at the time you're born, how long you're going to live is predestined.

River: I didn't take it that way. I think newer research shows that you can slow down the rate of cell division, and therefore, what'd she say about the clock?

Hannah: "Slow the hands of the clock."

River: Right. And live longer . . .

Mia: Well, I guess that's a good thing.

River: Yeah.

Take the Unit Test

1. What is the main topic of the lecture?
2. Which of the following was *not* mentioned as a way to slow aging?
3. What is the Hayflick Limit theory an example of?
4. What is the effect of reducing the amount of cellular waste?
5. What would the speaker probably say would happen to the food industry if many people adopted a CR diet?
6. How do free radicals cause cellular damage?
7. How can free radicals be reduced?
8. What kind of foods does the speaker recommend?
9. What would the speaker probably think about using medicines to extend life?
10. Why does the speaker prefer the natural approach?

Extend the Topic *page 110*

Sara: So, Professor Pirelli, I understand that you believe that our mental outlook can affect how long we live. Is that right?

Prof. Pirelli: Absolutely, Sara. We now have a lot of evidence that the mind-body connection is real. A positive or negative attitude can exert a strong effect on our health as well as our lifespan.

Sara: Is there any medical research to back up that idea?

Prof. Pirelli: Sure. First, positive emotions such as cheerfulness, liveliness, a "can do" attitude, and curiosity toward life can stimulate our brain to produce chemicals and hormones that strengthen our immune system and fight infection.

Sara: So having a positive attitude actually has a physical effect on us?

Prof. Pirelli: Yes, but there's more to it than that. People with a positive attitude have more of a fighting spirit, and that's particularly important when they have health problems. They're less easily defeated by those problems than more negative people. This attitude becomes more important as we age.

Sara: Because older people are more likely to have health problems.

Prof. Pirelli: Right. One last point is that people with a positive attitude follow their doctor's advice more often and more regularly than less positive people. For example, if their doctor tells them to take medicine or to exercise, they usually do it. You can imagine how important that can be.

Sara: Yeah, sure. OK, so there you have it. Want to live longer? Then stay positive. . . .

ANSWER KEY

Build Your Vocabulary *pages 103–104*

A. 1. a 2. c 3. a 4. b 5. c 6. c 7. b 8. b 9. a 10. a
B. Interact with Vocabulary! 1. Accumulating
2. accumulation of 3. accelerated 4. acceleration
5. nutrients 6. nutritious

Focus Your Attention *page 105*

A. *Sample notes:*

Problem	Solution
aging skin caused by overeating (meat, sweets)	switch diet: olive oil, fish, eggs, vegetables, fruit
aging skin caused by exposure to sunlight	avoid being outside from 10–4 during day; use sunscreen; wear hat

Listen for Main Ideas *page 106*

B. 1. Program theories 2. Damage theories 3. fifty
4. calorie restriction 5. imbalance 6. oxygen
7. high-tech, natural

Listen for Details *page 107*

B. 1. c 2. b 3. a 4. b 5. c 6. c 7. b

Talk about the Topic *page 108*

A. 1. Hannah 2. River, Manny 3. Manny
B. Asking for opinions or ideas: 3; Disagreeing: 2; Asking for clarification or confirmation: 1, 4

Review Your Notes *page 109*

Specific theory	Key terms	Causes of aging—Solutions
Hayflick Limit theory	cell division; cellular clock	Cause: our bodies are programmed to live a certain length of time Solution: reduce cell waste
No specific name given in lecture.	molecules; metabolic rate	Cause: free radicals cause damage to cell membranes and DNA Solution: metabolize less oxygen

Take the Unit Test

1. c 2. d 3. a 4. b 5. d 6. a 7. a 8. c 9. a 10. d

 **TEST** BIOLOGY: The Fountain of Youth

 Listen to each question. Circle the letter of the correct answer.

1. a. creating a healthy environment
   b. the process of cell division
   c. why people age
   d. increasing nutrition

2. a. decreasing cellular waste
   b. calorie restriction
   c. lowering the metabolic rate
   d. taking vitamins

3. a. a program theory
   b. a damage theory
   c. a mechanical theory
   d. a metabolic theory

4. a. New cells are produced more rapidly.
   b. Cells divide more slowly.
   c. Cell walls become stronger.
   d. Free radical damage is reduced.

5. a. It would grow rapidly.
   b. It would grow slowly.
   c. There would be little effect.
   d. It would be seriously damaged.

6. a. They damage DNA.
   b. They stop DNA from dividing.
   c. They destroy molecules.
   d. They cause an imbalance in stem cells.

7. a. by lowering the metabolic rate
   b. by using stem cells
   c. by eating high-calorie foods
   d. by exercising moderately

8. a. sweet desserts
   b. meat and fish
   c. fruits and vegetables
   d. natural grains

9. a. She would disapprove of them.
   b. She would strongly recommend their use.
   c. She would prefer procedures such as xenotransplantations.
   d. She would recommend using them in combination with a CR diet.

10. a. because it is the most economical
    b. because it is the easiest to implement
    c. because it is popular
    d. because it's her personal preference

TEACHING TIPS

UNIT OVERVIEW

In this unit, students work with different concepts related to marriage. The lecture focuses on two main benefits of marriage (the creation of social relationships among families and proper care for children) as well as the issue of who marries whom and why. In this part of the lecture, the focus is on *homogamy*, the tendency of people to marry someone similar to themselves in terms of race, level of education, and social class. The final part of the lecture concerns the changing face of marriage and the immediate future of marriage. Follow-up projects extend the topic to issues such as the effect of marriage on health, and personal qualities that contribute to successful marriages.

Connect to the Topic *page 112*   *~10 minutes*

As a warm-up activity, consider asking students to look at the Western and Eastern wedding photos and share their knowledge about those traditions. Another discussion could focus on trends in interracial relationships, depicted in the third photo. In the survey, students rank five characteristics of a potential marriage partner—good looks, kindness, wealth, nationality, and intelligence—in terms of their importance, then discuss as a class.

Build Your Vocabulary *pages 113–114*   *~15 minutes*

Students study the following words and phrases related to sociology and marriage:

adulthood	linked to	population
benefits of	mature	pregnant
confirmation (of)	matured	pressure for
confirmed	maturity	recognized by
couples	national	rise in
functions of	nationalistic	similar to
interracial	barriers	social class
legitimacy	nations	survival of
legitimately	norm	

After the Interact with Vocabulary! activity, you may want to have students practice using the boldfaced words with their partners. Knowing collocations can help students expand their vocabularies and increase their fluency.

Focus Your Attention *page 115*   *~10 minutes*

Students learn effective strategies for actively thinking about their lecture notes:

Add examples from your life.

Agree and disagree with information in the lecture.

Suggest an alternative point of view.

Consider the implications of information in the lecture.

Provide additional reasons for something.

Consider the strengths and weaknesses of a position or situation.

Predict how the situation will change in the future.

Listen to the Lecture *pages 116–117*   *~30 minutes*

Students consider benefits of marriage and criteria for choosing a partner (Before You Listen) before listening to the unit lecture on marriage. Students then answer multiple-choice items (Listen for Main Ideas) and true/false items (Listen for Details).
Lecture video time: 5 min. 46 sec.   *Number of episodes: 9*

Talk about the Topic *page 118*   *~20 minutes*

Four students—Michael, Yhinny, Qiang, and May—discuss the lecture. Part A focuses on matching these students with anecdotes from the discussion. In Part B, your students work on these discussion strategies:

- Expressing an opinion: "You know what I find fascinating . . . "
- Offering a fact or example: "Even here, generally, couples are expected to get married."
- Paraphrasing: "So in other words, in your parents' generation you see a lot of homogamy, but not in ours?"

For Part C, students are encouraged to use the discussion strategies they've learned. They may use phrases from the student discussion and/or the Discussion Strategy box, or come up with their own. Encourage students to provide reasons for their opinions and to elaborate on their responses.
Student discussion video time: 1 min. 23 sec.

Review Your Notes *page 119*   *~15 minutes*

Students focus on adding comments to their notes as a way of actively thinking about the ideas presented in the lecture.

BONUS ACTIVITY

As a lead-in to the unit test, you can supplement this activity by asking students to select five points from the lecture that they feel are important or interesting and to tell those points along with their personal reactions to a classmate.

Take the Unit Test *Teacher's Pack page 73*   *~15 minutes*

You may want to play the lecture again just before giving the test. Students answer standard test questions about the content of the lecture. Specifically, the test covers the following: the benefits of marriage, the alliance theory, the legitimacy argument, homogamy, the future of marriage, and the speaker's attitude toward interracial marriages.

Extend the Topic *pages 120–121*   *~30 minutes*

- Listening and Discussion: Students listen to a discussion on the effects of marriage on health, then discuss among themselves.
- Reading and Discussion: Students read and discuss three perspectives on the future of marriage.
- Research and Presentation: Students research and discuss the top ten personality characteristics considered important for a successful marriage.

Focus Your Attention:
Try It Out! *page 115*

Speaker: Although marrying someone who we love seems natural to many people, it's actually a rather new idea in the Western hemisphere. Up until about 300 years ago, many Europeans had a very different reason for marrying. Business! Traditionally, people in Europe lived in the same building where their business was located. And in these circumstances, marriages were often like business partnerships between a husband and wife. And you might be interested to know that this practice still exists in some parts of the world. However, as businesses gradually separated from the home, this economic reason for marriage, which was really a kind of external motivation, weakened. And it was replaced by internal motivations for marriage, such as personal feelings, desires, and personal preferences. OK, now let's take a look . . .

Listen for Main Ideas and Listen
for Details *pages 116–117*

Sociology lecturer: **E1** So my first question to you today is, "How would you define marriage?" Well, many people might say something like, "It's a union of two or more people who are legally recognized by the government," or "It's a couple that lives together and has and raises children." Sound good? Both of these ideas are true in many, but not all, cultures. Actually, most anthropologists, including myself, agree that there is no single definition that adequately describes all of the types of marriages found throughout the world. But whatever the definition, some form of marriage is found in every society, and I'd say that marriage serves an extremely important function in society. So let's first look at some of the benefits of marriage to society. **E2** Now a universal benefit of marriage is that it creates relationships or alliances among families. Now, some anthropologists believe that this is the main reason why marriage developed in human society. This idea is summed up in what is known as the alliance theory, which simply says that marriage increases social cooperation through the relations that develop between people and their in-laws. And this kind of human network is, in turn, good for society as a whole. **E3** A second benefit of marriage concerns children. Compared with animals, humans take an extremely long time to mature, from infancy until adulthood when they become independent. Because of this, children need parents to care for them for the first few years of their lives. And

marriage increases the likelihood that a child will be properly cared for and that the child will receive the support and protection of both parents over a long period of time. Obviously, this is quite important to the survival and development of a society. **E4** Now children also play a role in the third and final benefit we'll discuss. You see, in most cultures, marriage establishes the legitimacy and rights of a child because it establishes who the child's father is. Now, this is known as "the legitimacy argument," which says that in order for a child to be recognized and respected by the community, the child must be linked to a father who is legitimately married to the child's mother. This is particularly true in most modern societies, where there is a strong pressure for couples to get married if the woman becomes pregnant. However, I might add that this kind of pressure is lessening in some Western countries. All right, so I hope that we agree that marriage benefits society in many ways. **E5** Next I'd like to consider who marries whom and why. Any guesses? Well, statistics clearly show that most people marry someone similar to themselves in terms of race, level of education, social class, and interests. This social phenomenon is called homogamy. For instance, more than 90 percent of Americans marry someone from their own racial group, and about 75 percent marry someone from their same social class. **E6** Now, why is the phenomenon of homogamy so prevalent? Well, there's a very logical reason: People tend to marry people they've met in their daily lives, and most people tend to live near and socialize with people from their own racial group, their own social class, and with similar levels of education. I suspect that the many married couples you know confirms that homogamy is the norm. However, recent research suggests that this trend in marriage is changing and that marriages will look different in the future. **E7** To talk about the future of marriage, I'd like to focus on some figures from the U.S., although these ideas certainly apply to countries throughout the world. The strongest major trend that we'll see in marriages of the future is a gradual decline in racial homogamy. In 1980, 1.3 percent of marriages in the U.S. were interracial. By 2002 the number had risen to 3 percent, and by 2005 the number of interracial marriages had risen to 7.5 percent. So as you can see, this trend is accelerating rapidly, and we have many reasons to believe that the number of interracial marriages in the U.S. will continue to increase for some time to come. **E8** One reason is a rise in racial tolerance. A recent poll showed that 86 percent of blacks, 79 percent of Hispanics, and 66 percent of whites would accept their children or their grandchildren marrying someone of a different race. Another reason anthropologists believe interracial marriages will become more common is related to anticipated increases in the Hispanic and Asian populations in the U.S. These two groups account for many of the interracial marriages that we now see, so as these populations grow, we can assume so will interracial marriages. **E9** Now, I hope you'll agree that this trend is a very welcome one. Remember that one universal characteristic of marriage is that it creates alliances, and what better way to bring down racial and nationalistic barriers than through interracial and international marriages?

Coaching Tips

[1] Critical Thinking: Identifying point of view
How would you describe the speaker's feelings about marriage? It would be accurate to say he strongly supports it, right? His words "extremely important" tell us that. Keep his point of view in mind as you listen to the rest of the lecture. Knowing a speaker's point of view can help you keep a balanced perspective as you take in information.

Find audioscript for the other Coaching Tips at www.pearsonlongman.com/contemporarytopics.

Talk about the Topic *page 118*

Yhinny: It's funny—when I think of my parents and their married friends, they're all so similar. Just like the lecturer said. But people our age? It seems like I see a lot of diversity in the couples now.

May: Uh-huh.

Michael: So, in other words, in your parents' generation you see a lot of homogamy, but not in ours?

Yhinny: Yeah. I mean, I'm from a pretty conservative family, so my parents and people like them probably didn't want to challenge the norm, you know?

Michael: Yeah, well, I mean I grew up in New York City, and so there are a lot of mixed marriages there.

May: Like racially mixed?

Michael: Right. Yeah, OK, good point. So, maybe in the other ways, like education and class, those couples are still homogenous.

Qiang: You know what I find fascinating is that in many cultures, marriage seems to be less and less important every day. I mean, I know a lot of couples that are living together. But they're not even married.

May: Actually, where I'm from, that's totally unacceptable.

Yhinny: Really?

May: Yeah, people frown upon it, and no one talks about it openly.

Michael: Well, I think, even here, generally, couples are expected to get married, I mean especially if they're planning on having children.

Yhinny: Wow, I'd love to be a sociologist a hundred years from now and see what marriages look like then.

Qiang: Huh.

May: Oh boy.

Yhinny: I think big changes are ahead.

Michael: I think you're right.

Qiang: You don't have to wait that long.

Take the Unit Test

1. What are three benefits of marriage?
2. Which one of the following topics is *not* discussed in the lecture?
3. What is the central idea of alliance theory?
4. Why is protecting children an important role of marriage?
5. According to the legitimacy argument, who must the child be linked to?
6. What is it called when a person marries someone similar to themselves?
7. If you lived forty years in the future, what major change in marriage might you see?
8. Which of the following can we guess about the future of marriage?
9. What does the speaker think about marriage in general?
10. What is the speaker's attitude toward interracial marriages?

Extend the Topic *page 120*

Duke: Sharon, thanks so much for joining us today. You're here today to tell us about something that may surprise many of our listeners—that marriage is good for our health!

Sharon: Yes, Duke, it's really true. A major national study recently showed that married people are healthier in nearly every measure of health. Actually, about 40 percent of married people and only 25 percent of unmarried people in the U.S. say that they're "very happy" with their lives. And psychological health is known to be an important cause of physical health.

Duke: And do these benefits extend equally to both the husband and wife?

Sharon: Well, although both benefit, men clearly benefit more. For example, married men live an average of ten years longer than their unmarried counterparts.

Duke: Isn't that amazing? Now why is that?

Sharon: Well, in addition to the happiness issue, we know that married people tend to have stronger immune systems, closer family relationships, and less anxiety. They also tend to consume less alcohol and smoke less.

Duke: I see. So there's a whole host of reasons. Now do these findings only apply to the U.S.?

Sharon: No, not at all. The health benefits of marriage have been found in many cultures, and in many social groups. It's quite a widespread phenomenon, which, by the way, doesn't seem to apply to couples who simply live together. There really seems to be something important about making a legal commitment to one's partner.

Duke: Really? Fascinating . . .

ANSWER KEY

Build Your Vocabulary pages 113–114
B. 1. i 2. e 3. f 4. c 5. h 6. b 7. a 8. d 9. j 10. g
C. 1. N 2. V 3. A 4. N 5. V 6. N 7. N 8. N 9. A
10. N **D. Interact with Vocabulary!** 1. confirmed
2. confirmation 3. legitimately 4. legitimacy
5. mature 6. maturity 7. national 8. nations

Focus Your Attention page 115
A. in the Western hemisphere; many Europeans married for business reasons; in the same building; a business partnership; personal feelings, desires, and preferences

Listen for Main Ideas pages 116–117
B. 1. c 2. b 3. a 4. c 5. a 6. b 7. c

Listen for Details page 117
B. 1. F (there are many definitions) 2. T 3. T 4. F (father) 5. F (the same social class) 6. F (risen) 7. T

Talk about the Topic page 118
A. 1. Yhinny 2. Michael 3. Qiang **B.** Expressing an opinion: 2, 4; Offering a fact or example: 3; Paraphrasing: 1

Review Your Notes page 119
Sample reactions: **On social cooperation:** brings families together **On child care:** unmarried couples care for their children just as effectively as married couples v. children may be cared for by people other than their parents for most of the day **Establishment of children's legal rights:** society must carefully protect children's legal rights b/c they can't do so for themselves v. children should have the same legal rights whether parents marry or not **Marriage partner and social class:** people in cities can easily meet/marry people from a dif't social class v. many people are prejudiced toward those they believe are from a lower social class; this trend may be difficult to Δ **Marriage partner and racial group:** b/c most people can easily meet people from a dif't racial group at school/work, interracial marriages are possible v. racial prejudice = serious issue in many countries, so resistance remains **Marriage partner and educational level:** some people meet their spouse at college/job, so will probably marry someone w/similar education v. dif's in ed. level unimportant as long as the couple communicates well **Future of marriage and racial homogamy:** racial homogamy will ↑ b/c trend is toward internationalization v. racial homogamy may remain the norm in isolated areas

Take the Unit Test
1. b 2. c 3. b 4. c 5. b 6. c 7. a 8. d 9. a 10. c

 TEST SOCIOLOGY: Marriage

 Listen to each question. Circle the letter of the correct answer.

1. a. alliances of families, protection of children, rights of parents

   b. alliances of families, protection of children, identity of a child's parents

   c. alliances of children, protection of children, rights of parents

   d. alliances of children, protection of children, identity of a child's parents

2. a. the definition of marriage

   b. the legitimacy argument

   c. religious homogamy

   d. future trends of marriage

3. a. legal recognition

   b. social cooperation

   c. the development of society

   d. the legitimacy of children

4. a. because most families do not have many children

   b. because governments do little to protect children

   c. because humans mature slowly

   d. because brothers and sisters are unable to protect one another

5. a. the mother

   b. the father

   c. the grandparents

   d. the brothers and sisters

6. a. alliance theory

   b. legitimacy

   c. homogamy

   d. interracial marriage

7. a. less racial homogamy

   b. more divorces

   c. more racism

   d. fewer marriages

8. a. Some couples with children in Western countries will choose to not marry.

   b. The number of marriages will decrease sharply in many countries.

   c. Married couples will choose to have fewer children.

   d. The number of nontraditional marriages will increase.

9. a. It benefits society in many ways.

   b. It no longer serves a useful purpose.

   c. It must be changed.

   d. It's only useful in a few societies.

10. a. He appears to dislike them.

    b. He appears neutral.

    c. He appears to support them.

    d. He gives no indication of his opinion.